BASIC aerodynamics

D0705476

To Anne, Jane, David and Paul

BASIC aerodynamics

C B Stribling MBE, BSc, CEng, FIMA, MRAeS

Principal Lecturer
Royal Military College of Science, Shrivenham, England

Butterworths
London Boston Durban Singapore Sydney Toronto Wellington

First published 1984

© Butterworth & Co (Publishers) Ltd 1984

British Library Cataloguing in Publication Data

Stribling, C. B.
  BASIC aerodynamics.
  1. Aerodynamics—Data processing
  2. Basic (Computer program language)
  I. Title
  533'.62'0285422.4   QA930
  ISBN 0–408–01310–9

Library of Congress Cataloging in Publication Data

Stribling, C. B.
  BASIC aerodynamics.
  Bibliography: p.
  Includes index.
  1. Aerodynamics—Data processing   2. Basic
  (Computer program language)   I. Title
  TL573.S76 1984   629.132'3'0285424   84–14234
  ISBN 0–408–01310–9

Photoset by Butterworths Litho Preparation Department
Printed and bound in Great Britain by Anchor Brendon Ltd, Tiptree, Essex

This page is dedicated to the memory of the book's author, Barry Stribling, who died before publication.

Preface

The use of computers, in an ever increasing field of applications, continues to grow at a very rapid rate.

In particular, the machine's ability to perform large arithmetical and data handling tasks quickly and accurately has enabled enormous progress to be made in many branches of engineering and science, and computing is now in the curriculum of all university and college courses in these subjects; not the least important reason for this is that the exercise of writing a successful computer program is a great aid to students' understanding of the principles and procedures of their subject. It therefore makes good sense to integrate the teaching and applications of computing as closely as possible with a student's engineering studies, and it is the aim of this book to link computer programming with instruction in the fundamentals of aerodynamic theory.

Each chapter of the book, with the exception of the first, consists of a short text which contains a summary of theory in one area; this takes the form of an 'essay' which introduces the fundamental concepts and the appropriate governing equations. There follows a series of worked example computer programs. These are introduced by an explanation of the problem to be considered, and a program which solves this problem is then given, together with example computer runs; finally a section of notes explains the construction and operation of the program, and indicates the engineering lessons to be learnt. Chapters end with a set of exercise problems for the student to attempt.

The chapter topics are those which would form the basis of any course in aerodynamics. Chapter 2 introduces the fundamental principles governing fluid flow; Chapter 3 deals with stream and potential functions and Chapter 4 considers the boundary layer. Chapters 5 and 6 set out the main results of aerofoil section and wing theory and finally Chapter 7 is concerned with supersonic flow.

The book uses the BASIC (Beginner's All-purpose Symbolic Instruction Code) language. With the development of microcomputers which have built-in BASIC, this language has largely usurped FORTRAN as the most commonly used computer language for general use by engineers. It enables students to develop (i.e. write, run, correct errors and re-run) programs very rapidly, and even a complex exercise can be completed in a relatively short time, thus retaining interest and building confidence. Chapter 1 presents a summary of the language with comments, and the main commands and statements are listed.

The book does not attempt to describe the subject of aerodynamics in a comprehensive manner – there are many such books available. Neither, for the same reason, does this work cover the BASIC language in any detail. Rather, it is aimed at helping students both to become proficient in BASIC by using the language in an important field of engineering and to use computing as a means of mastering the subject of aerodynamics.

The author wishes to acknowledge the assistance and encouragement afforded by his colleague Mr P. D. Smith (Senior Lecturer at RMCS) without which the book would not have been written.

CBS
1984

Contents

Chapter 1

Introduction to BASIC

1.1 The BASIC approach

The programs in this book are written in the BASIC programming language. BASIC (Beginner's All-purpose Symbolic Instruction Code) was developed at Dartmouth College, USA as an easy-to-learn general-purpose programming language. It was originally intended for use on time-sharing computer systems, but it has gained widespread popularity as the main language associated with microcomputers. The language is not only easy to learn but is also particularly easy to use. It is very simple to write a program, type it into the computer, run it and correct any errors and then run it again to obtain the required output in a quite short time.

The main disadvantages of simple BASIC relate to its lack of structure (see Section 1.4) but this is not an important consideration for short programs such as those presented in the following chapters.

This book is not an instruction manual on BASIC. If such a book is required the reader is referred to the works in the bibliography at the end of this chapter or to one of the many similar works. This book does aim, however, to help in the learning of BASIC by applying it to a relevant engineering subject. This aim can be met by the reader studying the examples and perhaps copying them and running them with different data and inputs and then trying some of the problems.

Although not a BASIC manual, a short description of the grammar of simple BASIC is given below so that the reader may be able to clarify any language problem rapidly.

1.2 The elements of BASIC

1.2.1 Mathematical expressions

One of the main objects of the example programs in this book is to evaluate and operate on the equations that arise in aerodynamics.

1

These equations contain numerical constants and variables (e.g. x) and functions (e.g. sin). All numbers are treated identically whether they be integers (e.g. 36) or real (e.g. 36.1). An exponential form is used to represent large or small numbers (e.g. 3.61E6 represents 3.61×10^6). Numeric variables are represented by a suitable combination of letters or by letters followed by a digit (e.g. E or NEW3). On many computers π is directly available to the user either as PI or as a π key. (In this book PI has been used.) An operation such as a square root can be done by using an in-built function (e.g. SQR(X)). The argument in brackets (X) can be a number, a variable or a mathematical expression. For trigonometrical functions (SIN(X), COS(X), etc.) the argument is interpreted as being in radians. Other functions include a natural logarithm and its exponential (LOG and EXP respectively), ABS which selects the absolute value of the argument and INT which selects the integer part of the argument.

Mathematical equations also contain operators such as plus, minus, etc. These operators have a hierarchy in that some are performed by the computer before others. In descending order of hierarchy the operators are

to the power of (^)
multiply (*) and divide (/)
add (+) and subtract (−).

Thus, for example, any multiplication is carried out before any addition. The computer works from left to right in an expression if the operators have the same hierarchy. The use of brackets allows any of these operations to be overriden. Hence:

$$\frac{a + b}{3c}$$

becomes (A + B)/(3*C) or (A + B)/3/C.

1.2.2 Program structure and assignment

A BASIC program is a sequence of statements which define a procedure for the computer to follow. As it follows this procedure, the computer allocates values to each of the variables. The values of some of these variables may be specified by data that are input to the program. Others are generated in the program using, for instance, the assignment statement. This has the form:

line number   LET   variable = mathematical expression

where the word LET is usually optional and therefore omitted.

As an example, the root of a quadratic equation

$$x_1 = \frac{-b + \sqrt{b^2 - 4ac}}{2a}$$

may be obtained from a statement such as

100 X1 = (−B + SQR(B^2 − 4*A*C))/(2*A)

It is important to realize that an assignment statement is not itself an equation. Rather, it is an instruction to the computer to give the variable on the left-hand side the numeric value of the expression on the right-hand size. It is therefore possible to have a statement

50 X = X + 1

which increases by 1 the value of X. Each variable can have only one value at any time unless it is subscripted.

Note that all BASIC statements (i.e. all the program lines) are numbered. the line number defines the order in which such statements are executed.

1.2.3   Input

For interactive or 'conversational' programs the user specifies variables by inputting data in response to prompts from the computer as the program is running. The statement has the form

line number INPUT variable 1 [, variable 2, ...]

e.g.

20 INPUT A, B, C

When the program is run the computer prints ? as it reaches this statement and waits for the user to type values for the variables, e.g.

? 5, 10, 15

which makes A = 5, B = 10 and C = 15 in the above.

An alternative form of data input is useful if there are many data or if the data are not to be changed by the user (e.g. a range of Reynolds numbers). For this type of data specification there is a statement of the form

line number READ variable 1 [, variable 2, ...]

e.g.

20 READ A, B, C

with an associated statement (or number of statements) of the form

line number DATA number 1 [, number 2, ...]

e.g.

1 DATA 5, 10, 15

or

1 DATA 5
2 DATA 10
3 DATA 15

Data statements can be placed anywhere in a program – it is often convenient to place them at the beginning of the program so that they can be easily changed.

When using built-in data it is sometimes necessary to read data from their start more than once during a single program run. This is done using the statement

line number RESTORE

1.2.4   Output

Output of data and the results of calculations, etc. is implemented by using a statement of the form

line number PRINT list

where the list may contain variables or expressions, e.g.

200 PRINT A, B, C, A*B/C

text enclosed in quotes, e.g.

10 PRINT "INPUT A, B, C IN MM"

or mixed text and variables, e.g.

300 PRINT "PRESSURE IS"; P; "N/MM^2"

The items in the list are separated by commas or semicolons. Commas give tabulations in columns, each about 15 spaces wide, while a semicolon suppresses this spacing. If a semicolon is placed at the end of a list, it has the function of suppressing the line feed. If the list is left empty, a blank line is printed.

The necessity of using PRINT statements in association with both 'run time' input (to indicate what input is required) and READ/DATA statements (because otherwise the program user has no record of the data) should be noted.

As noted above, limited control over layout is provided by commas, semicolons and simple PRINT statements, but the number of decimal places is determined by the BASIC program's compiler default value. This is frequently too many, resulting in the printing of an untidy, confusing and mainly irrelevant mass of numbers. The PRINT USING statement permits precise control to be exercised over both layout and decimal digits, e.g.

    300 PRINT USING "12A, 2X, DD. DDD, 2X, 7A";
        "PRESSURE IS"; P; "N/MM ˆ 2"

The 12A and 7A specify the number of characters in the strings; the 2X's specify two spaces and the DD, DDD indicates two digits to the left and three to the right of the decimal point. If the same layout is required in several PRINT USING statements, then an IMAGE statement can be employed to control the format of them all, e.g.

    290 IMAGE 12A, 2X, DD, DDD, 2X, 7A
    300 PRINT USING 290; "PRESSURE IS"; P; "N/MM ˆ 2"
    310 PRINT USING 290; "TEM'TURE IS"; T; "DEG K"
    320 PRINT USING 290; "DENSITY IS"; RHO; "
        KG/M ˆ 3"

A # suppresses the linefeed in a print image.

1.2.5 Conditional statements

It is often necessary to enable a program to take some action if, and only if, some condition is fulfilled. This is done with a statement of the form

    line number IF expression 1 conditional operator expression 2
    THEN line number

where the possible conditional operators are

    $=$ equals
   $<>$ not equal to
    $<$ less than
  $<=$ less than or equal to
    $>$ greater than
  $>=$ greater than or equal to

For example, a program could contain the following statements if it is to stop when a zero value of A is input

```
20 INPUT A
30 IF A < > 0 THEN 50
40 STOP
50 . . .
```

In this example, note the statement

line number STOP

which stops the run of a program. The statement

line number END

should be used at the end of a program though this is not essential.

1.2.6 Loops

There are several means by which a program can repeat some of its procedure. The simplest such statement is

line number GO TO line number

This statement could be used with the conditional statement example above so that the program continues to request values of A until the user inputs zero.

The most common way of performing loops is with a starting statement of the form

line number FOR variable = expression 1 TO expression 2 [STEP expression 3]

where the step is assumed to be unity if omitted. The finish of the loop is signified by a statement

line number NEXT variable

where the same variable is used in both FOR and NEXT statements. Its value should not be changed in the intervening lines.

A loop is used if, for example, N sets of data have to be READ and their reciprocals printed, e.g.

```
10 READ N
20 PRINT "NUMBER", "RECIPROCAL"
30 FOR I = 1 TO N
40 READ A
50 PRINT A, 1/A
60 NEXT I
```

Loops can also be used to generate data. Consider the example (given below) of a simple temperature conversion program:

```
10 PRINT "CENTIGRADE", "FAHRENHEIT"
20 FOR C = 0 TO 100 STEP 5
30 PRINT C, 9*C/5 + 32
40 NEXT C
```

1.2.7   Subscripted variables

It is sometimes very convenient to allow a single variable to have a number of different values during a single program run. For instance, if a program contains data for several different flow rates in a duct, it is convenient for these to be called $Q(1)$, $Q(2)$, $Q(3)$, etc. instead of Q1, Q2, Q3, etc. It is then possible for a single statement to perform calculations for all the flow rates e.g.

```
50 FOR I = 1 TO N
60 V(I) = Q(I)/A
70 NEXT I
```

which determines the velocity of flow for each flow-rate.

A non-subscripted variable has a single value associated with it and if a subscripted variable is used it is necessary to provide space for all the values. This is done with a dimensioning statement of the form

line number DIM variable 1 (integer 1) [, variable 2 (integer 2), ...]

e.g.

```
20 DIM V(20), Q(20)
```

which allows up to 20 values of V and Q. The DIM statement must occur before the subscripted variables are first used.

On some computers it is possible to use a dimension statement of a different form, e.g.

```
20 DIM V(N), Q(N)
```

where the value of N has been previously defined. This form, when available, has the advantage of not wasting storage space.

1.2.8   Subroutines

Sometimes a sequence of statements needs to be accessed more than once in the same program. Instead of merely repeating these statements it is better to put them in a subroutine. The program then contains statements of the form

line number GOSUB line number

When the program reaches this statement it branches (i.e. transfers control) to the second line number. The sequence of statements starting with this second line number ends with a statement

line number RETURN

and the program returns control to the statement immediately after the GOSUB call.

Some computers can call subroutines by label, e.g.

150 GOSUB SUPERSONIC

The program then branches to the labelled line:

290 SUPERSONIC: X9 = Y8 + 1

Subroutines can be placed anywhere in the program but it is usually convenient to position them at the end, separate from the main program statements.

Another reason for using a subroutine occurs when a procedure is written which is required in more than one program. In subroutines it is sometimes desirable to use less common variable names (e.g. X9 instead of X) so that the possibility of the same variable name being used with a different meaning in separate parts of the program is minimized.

1.2.9   Other statements

(1) Explanatory remarks or headings which are not to be output can be inserted into a program using

line number REM comment

Any statement beginning with the word REM is ignored by the computer. On some computers it is possible to include remarks on the same line as other statements.

(2) Non-numeric data (e.g. words) can be handled by string variables. A string is a series of characters within quotes (e.g. "PRESSURE") and a string variable is followed by a $ sign (e.g. A$). String variables are particularly valuable when printed headings need to be changed.

(3) Multiple branching can be done with statements of the form

line number ON expression THEN line number 1 [, line number 2, ...]

and

line number ON expression GOSUB line number 1 [, line number 2, ...]

When a program reaches one of these statements it branches to line number 1 if the integer value of the expression is 1, to line number 2 if the expression is 2 and so on. An error message is printed if the expression gives a value less than 1 or greater than the number of referenced line numbers.

(4) Functions other than those built into the language such as SIN(X), etc. can be created by using a DEF statement. For example

10 DEF FNA(X) = X^3 + X^2

defines a cubic function which can be recalled later in the program as FNA (variable) where the value of this variable is substituted for X. A defined function is of use where an algebraic expression is to be evaluated several times in a program.

(5) Matrix operations may be available, so that addition, multiplication and inversion can be performed on one line e.g.

line number MAT(PROD) = MAT(A1)*MAT(B2)
line number MAT(B) = INV(A)

These last three statement forms have not been used in this book. Where matrix manipulation is necessary, e.g. in Example Program 6.3, the matrix operation is programmed line by line using a form of Gaussian elimination[1].

1.3 Checking programs

Most computers give a clear indication if there are grammatical (syntax) errors in a BASIC program. Program statements can be modified by retyping them completely or by using special editing procedures. The majority of syntax errors are easy to locate but if a variable has been used with two (or more) different meanings in separate parts of the program some 'mystifying' errors can result.

It is not sufficient for the program to be just grammatically correct – it must also give the correct answers. A program should therefore be checked either by using data which give a known solution or by hand calculation.

If the program is to be used with a wide range of data or by users other than the program writer, it is necessary to check that all parts of it function. It is also important to ensure that the program does not give incorrect yet plausible answers when 'nonsense' data are input. It is quite difficult to make programs completely 'userproof' and they become somewhat lengthy by so doing. The programs in this book have been kept as short as possible for the purpose of clarity and may not therefore be fully 'userproof'.

1.4   Different computers and variants of BASIC

The examples in this book use a simple version of BASIC that should work on most computers, even those with small storage capacity. Only single line statements have been used though many computers allow a number of statements on each line with a separator such as /. Multiple assignments may also be possible, e.g.

$$1000 \ A(0) \ = \ B(0) \ = \ C(0) \ = \ D(0) \ = \ 0$$

There is one important feature which distinguishes computers, particularly microcomputers with a visual display unit (VDU). This concerns the number of columns available across each line and the number of lines that are visible on the screen. Simple modifications to some of the example programs may be necessary to fit the output to a particular microcomputer.

Various enhancements of BASIC have been made since its inception – these have been implemented on a number of computer systems. The programs in this book could be rewritten to take account of some of these 'advanced' features. Advanced facilities include more powerful looping and conditional statements and independent subroutines which make structured programs easier to write. Expressed simply, structured programming involves the compartmentalization of programs and minimizes branching resulting from statements containing 'GOTO line number' and 'THEN line number'. Good program structure is advantageous in long programs.

1.5   Summary of BASIC statements

Assignment
LET   Computes and assigns value
DIM   Allows space for subscripted variables

Input
INPUT	Reads data from 'run-time' keyboard input
READ	Reads data from DATA statements
DATA	Storage area for data
RESTORE	Restores data to its start

Output
PRINT	Prints output list
PRINT USING	Prints output list in required format
IMAGE	Controls print format

Program control
STOP	Stops program
IF. . .THEN	Conditional branching
GO TO	Unconditional branching
FOR. . .TO. . .STEP	Opens loop
NEXT	Closes loop
GOSUB	Transfers control to subroutine
RETURN	Return from subroutine
ON. . .THEN	Multiple branching
ON. . .GOSUB	Multiple subroutine transfer
END	Last line of program

Comment
REM	Comment in program

Functions
SQR	Square root
SIN	Sine (angle in radians)
COS	Cosine (angle in radians)
ATN	Arctangent (gives angle in radians)
LOG	Natural logarithm (base e)
EXP	Exponential
ABS	Absolute value
INT	Integer value
DEF FN	Defined function

1.6   Reference

1. Mason, J. C., *BASIC Matrix Methods*, Butterworths, (1984).

1.7 Bibliography

The books noted below represent only a fraction of those available on BASIC programming.

1. Alcock, D., *Illustrating BASIC*, Cambridge University Press, (1977).
2. Forsyth, R., *The BASIC Idea*, Chapman and Hall, (1978).
3. Gottfried, B. S., *Programming with BASIC – Schaum's Outline Series*, McGraw-Hill, (1975).
4. Kemeny, J. G. and Kurtz, T. E., *BASIC Programming*, Wiley, (1968).
5. Monro, D. M., *Interactive Computing with BASIC*, Arnold, (1974).

Chapter 2
Elements of fluid mechanics

ESSENTIAL THEORY

2.1 Introduction

Matter can exist as a solid in which intermolecular bonds are strong and applied compressive, tensile and shear forces produce finite deformations; or as a liquid in which intermolecular bonding is weaker and, while compressive forces are resisted, shear forces can cause deformation indefinitely; or finally as a gas in which bonds are very weak and any applied force produces shape and volume changes. Liquids and gases are fluids and, despite their molecular structure, are assumed to be continuous at normal pressures and densities. A fluid may therefore be defined as matter which will deform continually and without limit under the action of an external resultant shear force, however small. In this book the principal working fluid will be air, a mixture of gases; aerodynamics is the study of gaseous flows through ducts (internal flow) and around solid bodies (external flow).

2.2 Properties of fluids

The principal properties which influence the dynamics of fluids are summarized in Table 2.1.

Table 2.1

Property	Symbol	SI unit	Definition
Density	ρ	kg/m^3	Mass per unit volume
Static pressure	p	N/m^2	Normal stress in a fluid as measured by a sensor which is stationary relative to the fluid
Static temperature	T	K	A measure of the mean kinetic energy of the fluid molecules
Dynamic viscosity	μ	kg/ms	Ratio of shear stress to strain (velocity gradient) in a fluid
Kinematic viscosity	ν	m^2/s	
Ratio of specific heats	γ	Non dim	C_p/C_v . $\gamma = 1.4$ for air
Speed of sound	a	m/s	Speed of weak pressure waves

2.2.1   Some equations relating the fluid properties

Equation of state

$$p = R\rho T \tag{2.1}$$

where R is the gas constant. For air, $R = 287\,\text{m}^2/\text{sK}$.

Isentropic Gas Law

$$p = k\rho^\gamma \tag{2.2}$$

Speed of sound

$$a^2 = \frac{\mathrm{d}p}{\mathrm{d}\rho} = \frac{\gamma p}{\rho} = \gamma RT \tag{2.3}$$

For air,

$$a = 20.04 \quad \sqrt{T}\,\text{m/s}. \tag{2.4}$$

Viscosity

Sutherland's empirical formula for viscosity gives a good approximation for μ over the temperature range, $100 < T < 300$

$$\mu = 1.458 \times 10^{-6} \frac{T^{3/2}}{T + 110.4} \tag{2.5}$$

2.3   Fluid statics

By considering the equilibrium of a small element of fluid at rest in a large volume, the rate of change of pressure p with vertical distance z (upwards positive) may be shown to be

$$\frac{\mathrm{d}p}{\mathrm{d}z} = -\rho g \tag{2.6}$$

For an incompressible fluid (ρ = constant), this integrates to

$$p_2 - p_1 = -\rho g(z_2 - z_1) \tag{2.7}$$

where p_1 and p_2 are pressures at vertical distances z_1 and z_2 above any selected datum level. From this equation may be derived the calibration equations of various types of manometer for measuring pressure differences.

2.3.1   The atmosphere

The atmosphere is the fluid through which many bodies of
aerodynamic interest move; it is essentially at rest and therefore
subject to Equations (2.1) and (2.6). In temperate latitudes,
measurements have established the following average sea-level
values for density, pressure and temperature

$$\rho_0 = 1.225 \text{ kg/m}^3,$$

$$p_0 = 1.013 \times 10^5 \text{ N/m}^2 \quad \text{and}$$

$$T_0 = 288 \text{ K} (= 15°C).$$

and it is also found that temperature falls linearly with altitude at a
lapse rate $L = 0.0065$ K/m in the lower atmosphere (troposphere)
up to 11 000 m (tropopause); in the upper atmosphere (stratosphere), the temperature is constant at 216.5 K (= −56.5°C). Thus

$$\begin{array}{ll} T = T_0 - Lz & \text{for } z \leqslant 11\ 000 \\ T = T_T & \text{for } z > 11\ 000 \end{array} \tag{2.8}$$

combining Equations (2.1), (2.6) and (2.8) gives:

For $z \leqslant 11\ 000$

$$\frac{p}{p_0} = \left(1 - \frac{Lz}{T_0}\right)^{g/RL} \tag{2.9}$$

$$\frac{\rho}{\rho_0} = \left(1 - \frac{Lz}{T_0}\right)^{g/RL - 1} \tag{2.10}$$

For $z > 11\ 000$

$$\frac{p}{p} = \exp\left(\frac{11\ 000 - z}{RT_T/g}\right) = \frac{\rho}{\rho_T} \tag{2.11}$$

where suffix T refers to tropopause conditions.

2.4   Basic fluid dynamics

2.4.1   Types of flow

Fluid flow is *steady* if the parameters of the flow (velocity,
pressure, etc.) at any point are invariant with time; in an *unsteady*
flow, parameters vary with time. In practice, all flows, except the
very simplest, contain some turbulence and are strictly unsteady
but if the unsteadiness is confined to small volumes of the flow, it
is convenient to use long-term average values to describe the
turbulent regions and to assume that conditions are steady

throughout. The choice of reference system used to measure velocities may determine whether a particular flow is steady or unsteady. Uniform flow is flow in which the fluid velocity vector is the same everywhere in the flow.

2.4.2. Fluid particle paths

The paths of fluid particles in a flow are described by the following:

(1) STREAMLINE: a path along which the fluid velocity is in the direction of the tangent to the line. There is no flow across a streamline.

(2) STREAMTUBE: a tube whose surface is composed of streamlines.

(3) PATHLINE: a line traced out by an individual particle in the fluid.

(4) STREAKLINE: a line traced out instantaneously by a succession of particles which have all passed through a particular fixed point.

In steady flow, streamlines, pathlines and streaklines are coincident but this may not be the case in unsteady flow.

The one-dimensional continuity equation

Mass continuity requires mass flow rate along a streamtube $\dot{m}$ to be constant:

$$\dot{m} = \rho A U = \text{constant} \tag{2.12}$$

where A is streamtube cross sectional area and U is average velocity. If the fluid is incompressible, the volumetric flow rate

$$Q = AU = \text{constant} \tag{2.13}$$

The one-dimensional momentum equation

Momentum is a vector quantity and Newton's second law, Force = Rate of change of momentum, may be applied to a component of fluid momentum in any direction.

Along the streamtube of Figure 2.1:

$$F_x = \text{Net force acting ON THE FLUID}$$

$$= \dot{m} \left(U_x(B) - U_x(A) \right) \tag{2.14}$$

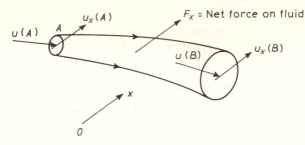

Figure 2.1 Velocities at two streamtube stations

where suffix x refers to components in some specified direction Ox, and U is average velocity. The net force will consist of pressure forces (acting inwards) at the end faces, pressure and shear forces acting on the fluid at the streamtube walls and fluid body forces such as weight.

The one-dimensional energy equation

If the fluid is inviscid, the equation of motion of an element of a streamtube may be expressed in the form

$$\frac{1}{\rho}\frac{dp}{ds} + g\frac{dz}{ds} + u\frac{du}{ds} = 0 \qquad (2.15)$$

where s is distance along the streamtube and z is distance above a reference level; this is Euler's equation. It applies along any streamtube and therefore, if the streamtube becomes infinitely thin, to the flow along a streamline.

Incompressible Bernoulli's equation

If density is constant, Euler's equation integrates to

$$p + \rho gz + \tfrac{1}{2}\rho u^2 = \text{constant} \qquad (2.16)$$

in which the first term is the static pressure, the second is the gravitational pressure and the third term is the dynamic pressure, often denoted q; the constant will also have dimensions of pressure and is called the stagnation pressure, the total pressure or the pitot pressure, depending on the application. When referring to the flow of air or other gases around a solid body, the vertical distance through which the air moves is usually small and the gravitational term may be neglected; incompressible Bernoulli's equation then becomes

$$p + \tfrac{1}{2}\rho u^2 = p_{ST} = \text{constant along a streamline} \qquad (2.17)$$

and it can be seen from this last equation that the stagnation pressure is the value of the static pressure at a point where the velocity is zero, i.e. at a stagnation point.

Compressible Bernoulli's equation

If pressure changes are isentropically related to density changes, i.e. $p = k\rho^\gamma$ then, neglecting the gravitational term again, Euler's equation integrates to

$$p \left(1 + \frac{(\gamma - 1)M^2}{2}\right)^{\gamma/\gamma-1} = \text{constant} = p_{ST} \qquad (2.18)$$

and for adiabatic conditions:

$$T \left(1 + \frac{(\gamma - 1)M^2}{2}\right) = \text{constant} = T_{ST} \qquad (2.19)$$

where $M = u/a$ is the Mach number.

The 'compressible' form of $q = \frac{1}{2}\rho u^2$ is $\frac{1}{2}\gamma p M^2$ $\qquad (2.20)$

2.5   Reynolds number and mach number

The equations of motion of a viscous compressible fluid (the Navier–Stokes equations) show that two separate flows which have geometrically similar boundary conditions (the same fluid/solid body boundary shapes) will be identical only if two similarity parameters, Reynolds number and Mach number, are the same for both flows.

Reynolds number

Reynolds number Re is defined as

$$\text{Re} = \frac{\rho UL}{\mu} = \frac{UL}{\nu} \qquad (2.21)$$

where L is a characteristic length. Re may be considered to be the ratio of inertia forces to viscous forces and therefore to be a measure of their relative importance; most external gaseous flows occur at a Reynolds number greater than 10^5 but internal flow Reynolds numbers are usually very much lower. The parameter is named after O. Reynolds conducted the well-known dye trace experiments on flow in pipes; these showed that, with similar boundary conditions throughout (the pipes were always circular in section), the type of flow, laminar or turbulent, was dependent on the value of the pipe Reynolds number. Reynolds number effects are important in all model testing.

Mach number

Mach number M is defined as

$$M = \frac{u}{a} \tag{2.22}$$

where u is fluid speed and a is speed of sound; these may be local or freestream values to give local or freestream Mach number. It may be considered to be the ratio of inertia forces to elastic forces, which are a measure of the compressibility of the fluid. Mach number effects are important in high-speed model testing.

All non-dimensional aerodynamic coefficients are functions of Re and M.

2.6 Dimensional analysis

Equations which relate physical quantities must be dimensionally consistent, a requirement which restricts the combinations of terms representing physical variables which can occur in an equation. This is the basic idea of dimensional analysis which is usually stated in the form known as Buckingham's Pi Theorem:

If a relationship is known to exist between N physical quantities, then it may be expressed as an equation relating $N - n$ independent, non-dimensional groups of variables (the Pi products) where n is the number of fundamental dimensions needed to specify the dimensions of the N variables.

2.7 Similarity and wind tunnel testing

As stated in Section 2.5, two flows with geometrically similar boundary conditions will be identical only if the flows are dynamically similar, i.e. Reynolds numbers and Mach numbers are the same. If this condition is satisfied, then non-dimensional aerodynamic coefficients will be the same. This principal indicates how scale models should be tested in order to simulate conditions in large-scale flows. Wind and water tunnels are frequently used to reproduce flow conditions around larger moving bodies totally immersed in a fluid, e.g. aircraft and submarines, but there are severe practical problems in reproducing exact dynamic similarity.

Wind tunnel corrections

The flow around a model in a wind tunnel is different from that which occurs in free air because of the constraints imposed on the flow by the tunnel walls and model supports. Tunnel measurements have therefore to be corrected to free air values to allow for changes in flow speed and direction and for streamwise gradients. The magnitude of these corrections depends upon the characteristics of the wind tunnel working section (e.g. its shape and size) as well as the dimensions of the model.

Balance corrections

Ideally, a wind tunnel balance used to measure up to six component forces and moments acting on a model would provide accurate values of all six variables. In practice, balance misalignment and transducer and signal processing errors introduce direct errors and cross coupling effects, so that, for example, a pure drag force on a model produces an erroneous drag reading as well as non-zero readings from the other five force and moment channels.

If true forces and moments, $X_1, X_2 \ldots X_6$ act on the model, then the measured balance outputs, $Y_1, Y_2 \ldots Y_6$ may be assumed to be linearly related to them by the matrix equation

$$\mathbf{Y} = \mathbf{AX} \qquad (2.23)$$

To calibrate a balance, known forces and moments, X, are applied one channel at a time and the outputs, Y, are noted; this procedure will find the matrix of coefficients, A. Subsequently, true forces and moments, X, may be obtained from balance readings, Y, by calculating: $\mathbf{X} = \mathbf{A^{-1}Y}$.

WORKED EXAMPLES

Example 2.1   ATMOS: atmosphere calculations

On a certain non-standard day, sea level temperature and pressure are found to be 21°C and $1.025 \times 10^5 \, \text{N/m}^2$ respectively and at 5000 m real altitude the temperature is −15°C; the lapse rate is constant. In the non-standard conditions, temperature, pressure and density variations with altitude are different from those of the standard atmosphere and an aircraft altimeter, calibrated and set for standard day conditions, will display an incorrect value for altitude.

The following program will (1) tabulate atmosphere conditions from sea level to 5000 m at 1000 m intervals on the non-standard day and (2) print a table which converts indicated altimeter readings into actual pressure altitude and give the error.

```
10      R=287
20      G=9.81
30      L=(21+15)/5000
40      P0=10250
50      T0=273+21
60      D0=P0/(R*T0)
70      PRINT "NON STANDARD DAY VALUES"
80      PRINT
90      PRINT " ALT        TEMP           DENSITY                PRESSURE"
100     PRINT " (M)        (DEG C)        (KG/M 3)               (N/M^2)"
110     PRINT
120     FOR Alt=0 TO 5000 STEP 1000
130       T=T0-L*Alt
140       P=P0*(1-(L*Alt/T0))^(G/(R*L))
150       D=P/(R*T)
160       PRINT Alt,T-273,D,P
170     NEXT Alt
180     PRINT
190     PRINT
200     PRINT "IND ALT      ACTUAL ALT             ERROR"
210     PRINT "  (M)          (M)                   (M)"
220     FOR H=0 TO 5000 STEP 500
230       Pr=10130*(1-(.0065*H/288))^(G/(R*.0065))
240       Z=T0/L*(1-(Pr/P0)^(R*L/G))
250       E=Z-H
260       PRINT H,Z,E
270     NEXT H
280     END
```

```
RUN
NON STANDARD DAY VALUES
```

ALT (M)	TEMP (DEG C)	DENSITY (KG/M 3)	PRESSURE (N/M^2)
0	21	.121477162293	10250
1000	13.8	.110698590282	9111.77808387
2000	6.6	.100638353053	8075.74476837
3000	-.6	.0912652378006	7135.00677297
4000	-7.8	.0825486267578	6282.97409924
5000	-15	.0744585011265	5513.35417441

IND ALT (M)	ACTUAL ALT (M)	ERROR (M)
0	101.165808313	101.165808313
500	610.007477753	110.007477753
1000	1118.22407667	118.224076671
1500	1625.80916934	125.809169338
2000	2132.75617786	132.756177857
2500	2639.05837731	139.05837731
3000	3144.70889067	144.708890674
3500	3649.7006835	149.700683498
4000	4154.02655833	154.026558328
4500	4657.67914886	157.679148862
5000	5160.65091382	160.650913818

Program notes

(1) Lines 10 to 60 state values of atmospheric parameters on the non-standard day; sea level pressure, temperature and density are P0, T0 and D0 respectively.

(2) Lines 120 to 170 contain a FOR loop which, starting from zero, increments the altitude, Alt, by 1000 until 5000 is reached. Within this loop are calculated and printed the non-standard day temperatures, densities and pressures using Equations (2.8) to (2.10).

(3) Lines 220 to 270 use a FOR loop again to compare indicated and actual altitudes from 0 to 5000. The indicated height, H, is used, at line 230, to calculate the pressure, Pr, being sensed by the standard altimeter. Line 240 finds the actual altitude, Z, where the pressure is Pr on the non-standard day. Line 250 finds the error, E.

(4) The printed results show that, on a non-standard day, altimeter error can be appreciable; in this example, the error increases with altitude.

Example 2.2   AIRSPEED: calculation of true airspeed and other speed-related parameters from air speed indicator readings

Instruments which tell the speed of an aircraft in flight require the stagnation and static pressures of the flow around the aircraft, and are calibrated according to some form of Bernoulli's equation. The calibration equation of the air speed indicator (ASI) is an approximation to the compressible form of Bernoulli's equation

$$p_p - p = \tfrac{1}{2}\rho_0 V_r^2 \left(1 + \frac{V_r^2}{4a_0^2}\right)$$

where $P_p = P_{ST}$ is the pitot pressure (the pressure in a forward facing pitot tube in which the air is brought to rest), p is atmospheric pressure, ρ_0 and a_0 are sea level values of air density and speed of sound and V_r is called the rectified airspeed (RAS). Clearly, V_r is not generally equal to the true airspeed (TAS) V, but V_r is a useful speed to the pilot because some performance and flying qualities are functions of RAS rather than TAS. For navigation, it is necessary to know TAS and this may be found from readings of the ASI, the pressure altimeter and the air thermometer (ASI errors are ignored).

The following computer program inputs values of V_r, pressure altitude and outside air temperature (corrected if necessary) and outputs the TAS, the Mach number M, the equivalent airspeed V_e defined by $V_e = V\sqrt{\rho/\rho_0}$, the dynamic pressure q, and the scale-altitude correction – the difference between V_r and V_e.

```
10      PRINT "PLEASE INPUT THE INDICATED AIRSPEED(M/S), THE PRESSURE"
20      PRINT "   ALTITUDE(M) AND THE OUTSIDE AIR TEMPERATURE(DEG C)"
30      INPUT Vr,Alt,T
40      PRINT Vr,Alt,T
50      PRINT
60      IF Alt>11000 THEN 90
70      P=101300*(1-.0065*Alt/288)^5.259
80      GOTO 100
90      P=22700*EXP((11000-Alt)/6334)
100     Pd=.5*1.225*Vr*Vr*(1+Vr*Vr/(4*340*340))
110     M=SQR(5*((Pd/P+1)^.2857-1))
120     V=M*20.04*SQR(T+273)
130     D=P/(287*(T+273))
140     Ve=V*SQR(D/1.225)
150     Q=.5*1.225*Ve*Ve
160     Sac=Ve-Vr
170     PRINT "TRUE AIR SPEED(M/S) = ";V
180     PRINT "MACH NUMBER = ";M
190     PRINT "EQUIVALENT AIR SPEED(M/S) = ";Ve
200     PRINT "DYNAMIC PRESSURE(N/M^2) = ";Q
210     PRINT "SCALE ALTITUDE CORRECTION(M/S) = ";Sac
220     END


RUN
PLEASE INPUT THE INDICATED AIRSPEED(M/S), THE PRESSURE
     ALTITUDE(M) AND THE OUTSIDE AIR TEMPERATURE(DEG C)
 100         0        15

TRUE AIR SPEED(M/S) =  99.9424713811
MACH NUMBER =  .293870588997
EQUIVALENT AIR SPEED(M/S) =  99.9653683424
DYNAMIC PRESSURE(N/M^2) =  6120.75835655
SCALE ALTITUDE CORRECTION(M/S) = -.0346316576049

RUN
PLEASE INPUT THE INDICATED AIRSPEED(M/S), THE PRESSURE
     ALTITUDE(M) AND THE OUTSIDE AIR TEMPERATURE(DEG C)
 300         1        15

TRUE AIR SPEED(M/S) =  298.278721589
MACH NUMBER =  .877057995341
EQUIVALENT AIR SPEED(M/S) =  298.329352181
DYNAMIC PRESSURE(N/M^2) =  54512.7464533
SCALE ALTITUDE CORRECTION(M/S) = -1.67064781891

RUN
PLEASE INPUT THE INDICATED AIRSPEED(M/S), THE PRESSURE
     ALTITUDE(M) AND THE OUTSIDE AIR TEMPERATURE(DEG C)
 100       15000      -56.5

TRUE AIR SPEED(M/S) =  234.71882714
MACH NUMBER =  .796015013285
EQUIVALENT AIR SPEED(M/S) =  93.4741922505
DYNAMIC PRESSURE(N/M^2) =  5351.67257784
SCALE ALTITUDE CORRECTION(M/S) = -6.52580774951
```

Program notes

(1) The operator inputs (at line 30) the values of rectified airspeed, pressure altitude and air temperature in response to the prompt which is printed by lines 10 and 20; these values are printed at line 40.

(2) Lines 60 to 90 calculate the atmospheric pressure, P, which the altimeter is measuring, using either the troposphere (2.9) or the stratosphere (2.11) equations as appropriate.

(3) Line 100 calculates the pressure difference, Pd, being sensed by the ASI using its calibration equation as given above in the introduction. This pressure difference and the atmospheric pressure are used in line 110 to calculate the Mach number, M, from a slightly modified form of Equation (2.19). True air speed, V, is then found at line 120 using (2.4), and density, D, equivalent air speed, Ve, dynamic pressure, Q and scale altitude correction, Sac, follow in succeeding lines.

(4) Outputs, with appropriate texts, are printed by lines 170 to 210.

(5) Three RUNs are shown. The first, at low speed and low altitude, shows that under these conditions, scale altitude correction is negligible and that rectified, equivalent and true air speeds are virtually the same. The second is at high subsonic speed and low altitude, showing that the scale altitude correction is small but not zero, and that equivalent and true airspeeds are the same at low altitude. The third at high altitude shows that the scale altitude correction is now quite significant, that there is a great difference between equivalent air speed (93 m/s) and true air speed (235 m/s) and that quite a low value of indicated airspeed (100 m/s) can be associated with a high subsonic Mach number of nearly 0.8.

Example 2.3   SPHDRAG: drag of a sphere

The results of tests to measure the drag force F on a smooth sphere of diameter D in air over a range of speeds V are:

Speed V (m/s)	Drag F (N)
4.94	0.16
7.41	0.38
9.89	0.64
12.36	0.98
14.81	1.38
17.28	1.80
19.76	2.29
22.25	2.78
24.71	3.20
27.18	2.85
29.65	1.62
32.12	1.89
34.58	2.14
37.07	2.40
39.49	2.71

Sphere diameter is 0.1524 m and air temperature and pressure are 17.5°C and 755 mm mercury respectively.

Dimensional analysis shows that the non-dimensional group $F/(\frac{1}{2}\rho V^2 S)$ – the drag coefficient C_d – is a function of $\rho VD/\mu$ which is sphere Reynolds number Re. S is sphere cross sectional area. The results of the experiment can therefore be displayed as a table of values of C_d against Re, and this table will then be applicable to all spheres under low speed conditions provided the Reynolds number is within the range tested.

The following computer program tabulates C_d against Reynolds number for the test results, and will then calculate the drag of a sphere of any combination of diameter, speed, fluid density and viscosity selected by the operator; this will generally require an interpolation between the actual test Re values. (Compressibility effects are ignored.)

```
10      DIM Re(15),Cd(15)
20      D=.1524
30      S=PI*D*D/4
40      T=273+17.5
50      De=755/1000*13600*9.81/(287*T)
60      Mu=.000001458*T^1.5/(T+110.4)
70      K1=.5*De*S
80      K2=De*D/Mu
90      DATA 4.94,.16,7.41,.36,9.89,.64,12.36,.98,14.81,1.38
100     DATA 17.28,1.8,19.76,2.29,22.25,2.78,24.71,3.20,27.18,2.85
110     DATA 29.65,1.62,32.11,1.89,34.58,2.14,37.07,2.40,39.49,2.71
120     PRINT "TEST RESULTS"
130     PRINT "------------"
140     PRINT
150     PRINT "REYNOLDS NUMBER    DRAG COEFFICIENT"
160     PRINT "---------------    ---------------"
170     FOR I=1 TO 15
180       READ V,F
190       Cd(I)=F/(K1*V*V)
200       Re(I)=K2*V
210       PRINT USING "5X,DDDDDD.15X,.DDD";Re(I),Cd(I)
220     NEXT I
230     PRINT
240     PRINT "DRAG OF A GENERAL SPHERE"
250     PRINT "------------------------"
260     PRINT
270     PRINT "DO YOU WISH TO CALCULATE THE DRAG OF ANY OTHER SPHERE? Y OR N. ";
280     INPUT A$
290     PRINT A$
300     IF A$="N" THEN 510
310     PRINT "PLEASE INPUT THE SPHERE DIAMETER AND SPEED (SI UNITS)    ";
320     INPUT D,U
330     PRINT D,U
340     PRINT "PLEASE INPUT THE FLUID DENSITY AND VISCOSITY (SI UNITS) ";
350     INPUT De,Mu
360     PRINT De,Mu
370     R=De*U*D/Mu
380     IF (R<Re(1)) OR (R>Re(15)) THEN 490
390     FOR I=2 TO 15
400       IF R>Re(I) THEN 480
410       R2=Re(I)
420       R1=Re(I-1)
430       Dc=Cd(I-1)+(Cd(I)-Cd(I-1))*(R-R1)/(R2-R1)
440       PRINT USING "5A,DDDDDD";"RE = ";R
450       PRINT USING "5A,.DDD";"CD = ";Dc
460       PRINT USING "14A,DDDD.DD,2A";"SPHERE DRAG = ";.5*De*U*U*PI*D*D/4*Dc;" N"
470       GOTO 260
480     NEXT I
490     PRINT "REYNOLDS NUMBER (";R;") OUTSIDE THE TEST RANGE; DRAG CANNOT BE CALCULATED."
500     GOTO 260
510     PRINT "END OF PROGRAMME"
520     END
```

```
RUN
TEST RESULTS
------------

REYNOLDS NUMBER      DRAG COEFFICIENT
---------------      ----------------
       50512              .595
       75769              .595
      101127              .594
      126383              .582
      151435              .571
      176691              .547
      202050              .532
      227510              .510
      252664              .476
      277920              .350
      303177              .167
      328331              .166
      353587              .162
      379048              .158
      403793              .158

DRAG OF A GENERAL SPHERE
------------------------

DO YOU WISH TO CALCULATE THE DRAG OF ANY OTHER SPHERE? Y OR N. Y
PLEASE INPUT THE SPHERE DIAMETER AND SPEED (SI UNITS)     .5  30
PLEASE INPUT THE FLUID DENSITY AND VISCOSITY (SI UNITS)  1.25           .0001
RE' = 187500
CD = .541
SPHERE DRAG =    59.72 N

DO YOU WISH TO CALCULATE THE DRAG OF ANY OTHER SPHERE? Y OR N. Y
PLEASE INPUT THE SPHERE DIAMETER AND SPEED (SI UNITS)     .2  10
PLEASE INPUT THE FLUID DENSITY AND VISCOSITY (SI UNITS)  .5  .005
REYNOLDS NUMBER ( 200 ) OUTSIDE THE TEST RANGE; DRAG CANNOT BE CALCULATED.

DO YOU WISH TO CALCULATE THE DRAG OF ANY OTHER SPHERE? Y OR N. N
END OF PROGRAMME
```

Program notes

(1) Line 10 declares 15 element arrays for storage of Reynolds numbers and drag coefficients; these will be required in the general sphere drag calculations in the second part of the program.

(2) Lines 20 to 60 give the test values of sphere diameter and cross sectional area, D and S, temperature, T, density, De, from the equation of state and viscosity, Mu, from Sutherland's formula. Lines 70 and 80 calculate two constants which are used at lines 190 and 200 to calculate Cd and Re.

(3) In this program, a DATA/READ combination of statements has been used to input the experimental results; these are at 90, 100, 110 and 180.

(4) A FOR loop carries out the processing of the 15 test readings between lines 170 and 220; Cd and Re are stored in arrays for future use. Results are printed with a PRINT USING statement at line 210.

(5) At line 270, the computer asks whether additional sphere drag calculations are required; if they are, the operator inputs information in response to prompts at lines 310 and 340. Reynolds number, R is calculated at 370 and checked to see if it is in the experimental range of Re at line 380; if it is not, line 490 prints a statement to this effect. The semicolons at the ends of lines 270, 310 and 340 suppress the normal carriage return operation.

(6) From 390 to 480, a FOR loop is used: (a) to find the test Reynolds number interval containing R – lines 400 to 420; (b) to calculate Cd at R by linear interpolation – line 430; and (c) to print results – lines 440 to 460.

(7) One RUN is shown. This tabulates the values of Re and Cd, and then performs two sphere drag calculations based on the test results; one of these is at a Reynolds number outside the test range.

Example 2.4   BALCAL: calibration of a three component wind tunnel balance

In a calibration test of a three component wind tunnel balance, known lift and drag forces and pitching moments are applied singly to the balance and the results are noted as follows:

Applied Forces and Moments X			Force and Moment Balance Readings Y		
Lift (N)	Drag (N)	P M (Nm)	Lift (N)	Drag (N)	P M (Nm)
+100	0	0	+98	+0.5	−0.2
0	+20	0	−0.2	20.4	+0.2
0	0	+10	−0.2	0	+9.7

Assuming that the balance readings Y (Y_1, Y_2, Y_3) are linearly related to the true forces and moments X (X_1, X_2, X_3) by the matrix equation

$$Y = AX$$

where

$$a_{ij} = \frac{\partial Y_i}{\partial X_j}$$

then the following program will calculate the values of the 9 coefficients a_{ij}, and then invert the matrix A so that true forces and moments can be found from measured readings which are input by the operator.

```
10    DIM X(3),Y(3),A(3,3)
20    PRINT "CALIBRATION TEST"
30    PRINT "----------------"
40    PRINT
50    J=1
60    PRINT "PLEASE INPUT THE APPLIED LIFT FORCE          ";
70    GOSUB 910
80    PRINT "PLEASE INPUT THE APPLIED DRAG FORCE          ";
90    GOSUB 910
100   PRINT "PLEASE INPUT THE APPLIED PITCHING MOMENT     ";
110   GOSUB 910
120   PRINT "MATRIX A IS:"
130   FOR I=1 TO 3
140     FOR J=1 TO 3
150       PRINT USING "DDD.DDD,5X,#";A(I,J)
160     NEXT J
170     PRINT
180   NEXT I
190   DIM B(3,6),C(3),Inv(3,3)
200   D2=1
210   FOR I=1 TO 3
220     FOR J=1 TO 3
230       B(I,J)=A(I,J)
240       IF I=J THEN 270
250       B(I,J+3)=0
260       GOTO 280
270       B(I,J+3)=1
280     NEXT J
290     C(I)=I
300   NEXT I
310   FOR I=1 TO 3
320     P=0
330     FOR J=1 TO 3
340       IF P>ABS(B(I,J)) THEN 370
350       P=ABS(B(I,J))
360       R=J
370     NEXT J
380     IF I=3 THEN 490
390     IF R=I THEN 490
400     D2=D2*(-1)
410     FOR J=1 TO 6
420       T=B(I,J)
430       B(I,J)=B(R,J)
440       B(R,J)=T
450     NEXT J
460     T=C(R)
470     C(R)=C(I)
480     C(I)=T
490     D=B(I,I)
500     D2=D2*D
510     FOR J=1 TO 6
520       B(I,J)=B(I,J)/D
530     NEXT J
540     FOR I1=1 TO 3
550       IF I1=I THEN 600
560       D=B(I1,I)
570       FOR J=1 TO 6
580         B(I1,J)=B(I1,J)-D*B(I,J)
590       NEXT J
600     NEXT I1
610   NEXT I
620   PRINT
630   PRINT "INVERSE OF MATRIX A IS:"
640   FOR I=1 TO 3
650     FOR J=1 TO 3
660       Inv(I,J)=B(I,J+3)
670       PRINT USING "DDD.DDD,5X,#";Inv(I,J)
680     NEXT J
690     PRINT
700   NEXT I
710   PRINT
720   PRINT "CORRECTION OF BALANCE READINGS TO TRUE VALUES"
730   PRINT "---------------------------------------------"
740   PRINT
750   PRINT "PLEASE ENTER READINGS OF LIFT, DRAG AND P.M."
```

```
760    PRINT "   ENTER 0,0,0 TO TERMINATE THE PROGRAMME"
770    INPUT Y(1),Y(2),Y(3)
780    PRINT Y(1),Y(2),Y(3)
790    IF Y(1)=0 AND Y(2)=0 AND Y(3)=0 THEN 1020
800    FOR I=1 TO 3
810      X(I)=0
820      FOR J=1 TO 3
830        X(I)=X(I)+Inv(I,J)*Y(J)
840      NEXT J
850    NEXT I
860    PRINT
870    PRINT "TRUE LIFT = ";X(1)
880    PRINT "TRUE DRAG = ";X(2)
890    PRINT "TRUE P M = ";X(3)
900    GOTO 730
910      INPUT X0
920      PRINT X0
930      PRINT "PLEASE INPUT THE MEASURED LIFT, DRAG AND P M ";
940      INPUT Y(1),Y(2),Y(3)
950      PRINT Y(1),Y(2),Y(3)
960      FOR I=1 TO 3
970        A(I,J)=Y(I)/X0
980      NEXT I
990      PRINT
1000     J=J+1
1010     RETURN
1020   PRINT "END OF PROGRAMME"
1030   END
```

```
RUN
CALIBRATION TEST
----------------

PLEASE INPUT THE APPLIED LIFT FORCE            100
PLEASE INPUT THE MEASURED LIFT, DRAG AND P M    98    .5        -.2

PLEASE INPUT THE APPLIED DRAG FORCE            20
PLEASE INPUT THE MEASURED LIFT, DRAG AND P M   -.2   20.4       .2

PLEASE INPUT THE APPLIED PITCHING MOMENT       10
PLEASE INPUT THE MEASURED LIFT, DRAG AND P M   -.2   0          9.7

MATRIX A IS:
    .980        -.010       -.020
    .005        1.020       0.000
   -.002         .010        .970

INVERSE OF MATRIX A IS:
   1.020         .010        .021
   -.005         .980       -0.000
    .002        -.010       1.031

CORRECTION OF BALANCE READINGS TO TRUE VALUES
---------------------------------------------

PLEASE ENTER READINGS OF LIFT, DRAG AND P M.
   ENTER 0,0,0 TO TERMINATE THE PROGRAMME
 50          10        -15

TRUE LIFT =  50.802444301
TRUE DRAG =  9.55488997892
TRUE P M = -15.4576742383
---------------------------------------------

PLEASE ENTER READINGS OF LIFT, DRAG AND P M.
   ENTER 0,0,0 TO TERMINATE THE PROGRAMME
 0           0         0
END OF PROGRAMME
```

Program notes

(1) Line 10 declares dimensions of the arrays X, Y and A which, respectively, will store true forces and moments, measured forces and moments and the matrix relating them. Line 190 also carries a DIM statement defining arrays to be used in the matrix inversion.

(2) Lines 50 to 110 and the subroutine 910 to 1010 input, using several printed prompts, the true and measured lift, drag and pitching moments used in the calibration test. The subroutine also calculates the values of the elements of matrix A and these are printed by lines 130 to 180.

(3) Lines 190 to 610 invert the matrix A using the method described in Chapter 1. If a matrix inversion facility is available, these 43 statements may be replaced by a single line e.g. Inv=MATINV(A). Lines 630 to 700 print the inverse which is now stored in Inv(3,3).

(4) The second part of the program commences at line 720 and, in response to a prompt at line 750, the operator inputs measured values of balance forces and moments; values of 0,0,0 are arranged to stop the program. Lines 800 to 850 calculate, by matrix multiplication of Inv and Y, the true values which are printed at 870 to 890.

(5) There is one RUN with one example of the conversion of measured balance readings to true readings.

(6) In order to avoid too long a program, it has been written to support a calibration test which uses only ONE set of lift, drag and PM values. In a serious balance calibration test, it would be preferable to apply several different values of each quantity and then determine best regression line slopes for the coefficients a_{ij}. An extension of the program to do this is suggested as a useful exercise for the student.

PROBLEMS

(**2.1**) Write a program which will input airspeed and then tabulate Reynolds number per unit length and Mach number over a range of altitudes from sea level to 20 km at intervals of 2 km.

(**2.2**) In order to simulate viscous effects in the flow around a full size aircraft correctly, model tests are sometimes conducted in pressurized wind tunnels in order to obtain a sufficiently high Reynolds number. Write a program which will input full-scale aircraft wing span, speed and altitude and which will then tell the wind tunnel engineer the pressure at which the tunnel should be run for dynamic similarity. The tunnel working section cannot accept models of span greater than 1 m without excessive interference effects and the tunnel maximum speed is 80 m/s. The program should print an appropriate statement if dynamic similarity cannot be achieved below the tunnel maximum working section pressure of 20 atmospheres.

(2.3) Aircraft altimeters, airspeed indicators and Machmeters, which rely on pressures sensed by the aircraft's pitot static system, are subject to errors (called pressure errors) as a result of errors in the measurement of atmospheric static pressure (pitot pressure is usually accurately sensed). As it is sometimes important for aircrew to know the aircraft's speed as accurately as possible, a table is provided which gives airspeed indicator errors at several airspeed indicator readings (ASIRs); such a table for one particular aircraft is as follows:

ASIR (m/s)	50	100	150	200	250	300
ASIR PRES ERR (m/s)	+2	+1	0	−1	−2	−3
TRUE V_r (m/s)	52	101	150	199	248	297

Write a computer program which will store this information on pressure error variation with ASIR, and which will input indicated pressure altitude and ASIR and give the following outputs:

(1) Pressure error and true V_r;
(2) The corrected pressure altitude;
(3) The corrected Machmeter reading.

The calibration equations of the altimeter, the ASI and the Machmeter are, respectively, Equations (2.9) or (2.11), the equation given in Example 2.2 and Equation (2.18).

(2.4) Write a program which will input a combination of any three of the four pipe flow parameters: fluid density, fluid viscosity, fluid speed and pipe diameter, and which will output the maximum or minimum value of the fourth parameter which will ensure that the flow in the pipe is laminar, i.e. Pipe Reynolds number <2000.

(2.5) An intermittent supersonic wind tunnel sucks in atmospheric air, accelerates it to supersonic speed through a throat upstream of the working section and exhausts it into a large vacuum tank. The working section cross sectional area is $0.025 \, m^2$. Write a program which will input atmospheric pressure and temperature and the required working section Mach number, and which will output the throat area and the working section pressure, temperature, density, speed and Reynolds number per unit length. The flow may be assumed isentropic.

(2.6) When fluid flowing in a pipe enters a bend there is a force exerted by the pipe walls on the fluid causing it to deflect. There is an equal and opposite force on the bend which must be adequately restrained by external clamps and brackets, etc.

Write a program which will evaluate the forces on tapered pipe bends carrying incompressible fluids and then modify the program to allow the operator to select for incompressible or compressible subsonic conditions.

(2.7) The presence of a model in the test section of a wind tunnel reduces the area through which the air may flow and hence, by continuity, increases the velocity of the air flowing over the model. This increase in velocity may be assumed constant over normal sized models and is known as 'solid blocking'. It is given by the equation $\Delta V = \epsilon V$ where ΔV is the velocity increase, V is the uncorrected velocity and ϵ is the blockage factor given by

$$\epsilon = \lambda\tau(A/C)^{3/2}$$

where λ is a factor depending on the shape of the body (typical value 5), τ is a factor depending on the tunnel cross section shape (0.8 for a closed jet circular or square tunnel), A is maximum cross sectional area of the body and C is the cross sectional area of the tunnel.

Write a program which will input any necessary values of the parameters defined above and output corrected values of tunnel speed.

Chapter 3

Stream function and velocity potential

ESSENTIAL THEORY

3.1 Fluid properties and flow conditions

All real fluids are viscous and compressible but there are many real flows of interest which are steady and in which viscosity and compressibility play a negligible part in the dynamics. In these conditions the problem of explaining fluid motion and some of the resulting interactions with solid bodies may be simplified by postulating that the fluid is inviscid, incompressible and time invariant. The results of an analysis carried out with these assumptions give valuable insight into the behaviour of real fluids and are often very close to those observed. The inviscid assumption will restrict the regions of flow that may be examined to those outside boundary layers and areas of separation, and the incompressible assumption requires the fluid velocity to be much less than the speed of sound; this last restriction is generally satisfied in normal liquid flows and in low-speed gas flows at a Mach number less than about 0.3. The following theory applies to steady, non-viscous, incompressible flows and will be restricted to two-dimensional conditions.

Streamlines

In steady flow, streaklines and pathlines coincide with streamlines which are described by the Cartesian equation $dx/u = dy/v$ and by the polar equation $dr/q_r = r d\theta/q_\theta$. The magnitude of the fluid velocity vector is $q = (u^2 + v^2)^{1/2} = (q + q_\theta^2)^{1/2}$.

Continuity

The principle of conservation of mass in a continuous fluid leads to the equation

$$\frac{\partial u}{\partial x} + \frac{\partial v}{\partial y} = 0 \tag{3.1}$$

and, in polar coordinates

$$\frac{\partial q_r}{\partial r} + \frac{q_r}{r} + \frac{1}{r}\frac{\partial q_\theta}{\partial \theta} = 0 \qquad (3.2)$$

Stagnation points

Flows frequently contain points at which the fluid is brought to rest. Such points are called stagnation points with local $u = v = q_r = q_\theta = 0$; at a stagnation point, streamlines may intersect.

Dividing streamlines

Streamlines through stagnation points are often important dividing lines between different regions of flow and they are called dividing streamlines.

Pressure coefficient

The non-dimensional difference in pressure between local (p and q) and freestream (P and U) conditions is the pressure coefficient

$$C_p = (p - P)/\tfrac{1}{2}\rho U^2 \qquad (3.3)$$

$$= 1 - q^2/U^2 \text{ for incompressible flow} \qquad (3.4)$$

$C_p = +1$ at a stagnation point ($q = 0$) and it is zero where pressure and velocity are equal to freestream values.

Force coefficients

The resultant force F, and its components X and Y, acting on a solid body may be obtained, in the absence of surface shear stresses, by integrating the pressure forces over the surface of the body. The resulting force coefficients C_X and C_Y are given by:

$$C_X = X/\tfrac{1}{2}\rho U^2 c = \int_S C_p \, \mathrm{d}(y/c) \qquad (3.5)$$

$$C_Y = Y/\tfrac{1}{2}\rho U^2 c = -\int_S C_p \, \mathrm{d}(x/c) \qquad (3.6)$$

where c is a convenient reference length and the integration extends over the body surface S.

3.2   The stream and potential functions

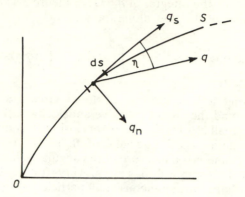

Figure 3.1 Velocity components at a small element ds of path OS

Consider, in Figure 3.1, the flux or rate of flow of fluid across a line joining a reference point O to a general point S in the fluid. This flow rate, ψ, will be a function of the coordinates of S and will be independent of the path joining O to S. ψ is called the *stream function* of the flow and from the physical definition:

$$\psi = \int_O^S q_n \, ds = \int_O^S q \sin \eta \, ds \tag{3.7}$$

ψ is constant along a streamline.

The value of the function

$$\phi = \int_O^S q_s \, ds = \int_O^S q \cos \eta \, ds \tag{3.8}$$

will, in general, depend on the integration path from O to S, but if the flow is irrotational (see Section 3.3), then it is dependent on the position of S only and is called the *potential function* of the flow.

Velocity components

The Cartesian (u, v) and polar (q_r, q_θ) velocity components may be obtained from ϕ or ψ

$$u = \partial\phi/\partial x = \partial\psi/\partial y \quad \text{and} \quad v = \partial\phi/\partial y = -\partial\psi/\partial x \tag{3.9}$$

$$q_r = \partial\phi/\partial r = 1/r\partial\psi/\partial\theta \quad \text{and} \quad q_\theta = 1/r\partial\phi/\partial\theta = -\partial\psi/\partial r \tag{3.10}$$

3.3   Circulation and vorticity

In a general flow, the integral of $q_s\mathrm{d}s$ (see Figure 3.1) along a line RS is a measure of the flow along the line, i.e.

$$\text{Flow along a line } RS = \int_R^S q_s\mathrm{d}s = \int_R^S q\cos\eta\,\mathrm{d}s \quad (3.11)$$

The flow along a line forming a closed circuit is called the *circulation* around the circuit (positive anticlockwise).

Consider a small elementary circuit enclosing an area δA around which the circulation is $\delta\Gamma$. The value of $\delta\Gamma/\delta A$ as $\delta A \to 0$ is called the *vorticity*, ζ, and it is a measure of the angular velocity, or spin, within a fluid. This spin will, in general, vary with position, unlike a solid body where, instantaneously, all particles are rotating with the same angular velocity. In terms of velocity components:

$$\zeta = \frac{\partial v}{\partial x} - \frac{\partial u}{\partial y} = \frac{\partial q_\theta}{\partial r} + \frac{q_\theta}{r} - \frac{1}{r}\frac{\partial q_r}{\partial\theta} \quad (3.12)$$

and the stream function ψ satisfies $\nabla^2\psi = -\zeta$ where ∇^2 is the Laplacian operator. Vorticity is related to the rate of change of stagnation pressure across streamlines:

$$\partial p_{st}/\partial n = \rho\zeta q \quad (3.13)$$

where n is the direction perpendicular to the local streamline. A flow over which vorticity is everywhere zero is said to be *irrotational*. In an irrotational flow, stagnation pressure is universally constant and both stream and potential functions satisfy Laplace's equation:

$$\nabla^2\psi = \nabla^2\phi = 0 \quad (3.14)$$

The integral (3.11) will have a value which is independent of the path between R and S only if the fluid vorticity is everywhere zero; i.e. the fluid is irrotational. The potential function (Equation (3.8)) is, therefore, single valued only in irrotational flows; it does not exist in the boundary layer but the stream function does.

3.4   Elementary stream and potential functions

The stream and corresponding potential functions of some simple flows are shown in Table 3.1.

Table 3.1

Flow	Stream function	Potential function
Uniform stream	U_y	U_x
Source	$m\theta/2\pi$	$m\ln r/2\pi$
Doublet with Axis along $+O_x$	$\dfrac{\mu y}{2\pi(x^2 + y^2)}$	$\dfrac{-\mu x}{2\pi(x^2 + y^2)}$
Free vortex	$-\Gamma\ln r/2\pi$	$\Gamma\theta/2\pi$
Forced vortex	$-\omega r^2/2$	Does not exist because $\zeta = 2\omega \neq 0$
Rankine vortex	$\begin{cases} -\omega r^2/2 & \text{within core radius } R \\ -\Gamma\ln r/2 & \text{outside core radius} \end{cases}$ with $\Gamma = 2\pi\omega R^2$	

The principle of superposition

The stream and potential functions of the vector sum of two or more flows are equal to the sum of the separate stream and potential functions.

3.5   Cylinder with circulation

The aerodynamically important flow of a uniform stream (U) around a cylinder (radius a) with circulation Γ has a stream function:

$$\psi = Ur \sin\theta\,(1 - a^2/r^2) + \Gamma \ln (r/a)/2\pi \qquad (3.15)$$

(The vortex has been chosen to rotate in a clockwise direction and is therefore preceded by a $+$ sign.)

Velocities are

$$q_r = U\cos\theta\,(1 - a^2/r^2) \quad \text{in general} \qquad (3.16)$$

$$= 0 \quad \text{on the surface of the cylinder} \qquad (3.17)$$

$$q_\theta = -U\sin\theta\,(1 + a^2/r^2) - \Gamma/2\pi r \quad \text{in general} \qquad (3.18)$$

$$= -2U\sin\theta - \Gamma/2\pi a \quad \text{on the cylinder surface} \qquad (3.19)$$

Two stagnation points occur on the cylinder surface at

$$\theta = \sin^{-1}(-\Gamma/4\pi aU) \quad \text{provided } |\Gamma| < 4\pi aU \qquad (3.20)$$

On the cylinder surface, the pressure coefficient is

$$C_p = 1 - (2\sin\theta + \Gamma/2\pi aU)^2 \qquad (3.21)$$

and the force coefficients, obtained by surface pressure integration, are

$$C_X = 0 - \text{d'Alembert's paradox} \qquad (3.22)$$

$$C_Y = \rho U \Gamma \qquad (3.23)$$

This last equation is a most important result, known as the Kutta Joukowski theorem. It shows that if circulation can be introduced into the flow around a cylinder, then a LIFT force – that is a force perpendicular to the free stream direction – is produced. A cylinder spinning about its own axis in a real fluid will create a circular flow as a result of viscous effects and it will consequently experience a lift force (either vertical or horizontal depending on the orientation of the axis relative to the freestream) when it moves through the fluid; this phenomena is called the Magnus effect. Equations (3.22) and (3.23) also apply to two-dimensional closed shapes other than cylinders; in particular, to aerofoil sections.

WORKED EXAMPLES

Example 3.1   STRFUNC: evaluation of the stream function

This simple program evaluates the stream function at a general point, (x, y) in the flow resulting from placing a source of strength m in a stream of speed U. The stream function is given by: $\psi = U_y + m\theta/2\pi$.

```
10      PRINT "PLEASE INPUT THE UNIFORM STREAM VELOCITY AND SOURCE STRENGTH"
20      INPUT U,M
30      PRINT "PLEASE INPUT THE COORDINATES OF THE POINT AT WHICH THE VALUE"
40      PRINT "      OF THE STREAM FUNCTION IS TO BE CALCULATED"
50      INPUT X,Y
60      IF X=0 THEN 90
70      T=ATN(Y/X)
80      GOTO 100
90      T=PI/2*SGN(Y)
100     IF X>=0 THEN 130
110     T=T+PI
120     GOTO 150
130     IF Y>=0 THEN 150
140     T=T+2*PI
150     S1=M*T/2/PI
160     S2=U*Y
170     S=S1+S2
180     PRINT
190     PRINT "UNIFORM STREAM = ";U;" M/S"
200     PRINT "SOURCE STRENGTH = ";M;" M^2/S"
210     PRINT "STREAM FUNCTION VALUE AT (";X;Y;") IS ";S;" M^2/S"
220     PRINT
230     PRINT "DO YOU WISH TO DO MORE CALCULATIONS;  INPUT Y OR N"
240     INPUT A$
250     PRINT A$
260     PRINT
270     PRINT
280     PRINT
290     IF A$="Y" OR A$="y" THEN 10
300     PRINT
310     PRINT "END OF PROGRAMME"
320     END
```

```
RUN
PLEASE INPUT THE UNIFORM STREAM VELOCITY AND SOURCE STRENGTH
PLEASE INPUT THE COORDINATES OF THE POINT AT WHICH THE VALUE
     OF THE STREAM FUNCTION IS TO BE CALCULATED

UNIFORM STREAM =  5  M/S
SOURCE STRENGTH =  20  M^2/S
STREAM FUNCTION VALUE AT ( 5   5 ) IS   27.5  M^2/S

DO YOU WISH TO DO MORE CALCULATIONS: INPUT Y OR N
Y


PLEASE INPUT THE UNIFORM STREAM VELOCITY AND SOURCE STRENGTH
PLEASE INPUT THE COORDINATES OF THE POINT AT WHICH THE VALUE
     OF THE STREAM FUNCTION IS TO BE CALCULATED

UNIFORM STREAM =  5  M/S
SOURCE STRENGTH =  20  M^2/S
STREAM FUNCTION VALUE AT (-4   4 ) IS   27.5  M^2/S

DO YOU WISH TO DO MORE CALCULATIONS: INPUT Y OR N
Y


PLEASE INPUT THE UNIFORM STREAM VELOCITY AND SOURCE STRENGTH
PLEASE INPUT THE COORDINATES OF THE POINT AT WHICH THE VALUE
     OF THE STREAM FUNCTION IS TO BE CALCULATED

UNIFORM STREAM =  100  M/S
SOURCE STRENGTH =  20  M^2/S
STREAM FUNCTION VALUE AT (-10   0 ) IS   10  M^2/S

DO YOU WISH TO DO MORE CALCULATIONS: INPUT Y OR N
N


END OF PROGRAMME
```

Program notes

(1) In lines 10 to 50, the operator inputs the uniform stream speed and the source strength, and selects the point at which the stream function is to be evaluated.

(2) It is necessary to calculate the correct value for θ from the given Cartesian coordinates, x, y. All computers carry an ATN function but the output in radians is usually presented in the range $-\pi/2$ to $+\pi/2$. Lines 60 to 140 produce the correct value for θ between 0 and 2π.

(3) Lines 150 to 170 calculate the stream function, S, and 180 to 210 give the output.

(4) Note that the stream function has the same value in the first two program runs; the points $(5,5)$ and $(-4,4)$, therefore, lie on the same streamline. As a STUDENT EXERCISE, find, by trial and error, other points on this streamline.

(5) To evaluate the stream function of a different flow, replace statements 150 to 170 by statements defining the new stream function.

Example 3.2   STRCOORDS: streamlines of a source in a uniform stream

This program considers the external flow (flow outside the dividing streamline) of a source in a uniform stream. At a series of predetermined x coordinate values, ranging from a large distance upstream to a large distance downstream of the source, the corresponding y coordinate on a selected streamline is calculated; these coordinates, together with fluid speed and pressure coefficient, are tabulated.

```
10      PRINT "PLEASE INPUT THE UNIFORM STREAM SPEED AND THE SOURCE STRENGTH"
20      INPUT U,M
30      PRINT U,M
40      PRINT "PLEASE INPUT THE STREAM FUNCTION OF THE SELECTED STREAMLINE"
50      PRINT "IT MUST BE GREATER THAN OR EQUAL TO M/2 WHERE M IS SOURCE STRENGTH"
60      INPUT P
70      IF P<M/2 THEN 40
80      PRINT P
90      PRINT
100     D=M/(2*PI*U)
110     PRINT "THE STAGNATION POINT IS: D = ";D;" METRES UPSTREAM OF THE SOURCE"
120     PRINT
130     PRINT "MULTIPLE OF D   X COORD    Y COORD     VELOCITY    PRESSURE COEFFT"
140     PRINT "-------------   -------    -------     --------    ---------------"
150     X=-25
160     GOSUB 360
170     X=-10
180     GOSUB 360
190     FOR X=-5 TO -2
200        GOSUB 360
210     NEXT X
220     FOR X=-1.5 TO .5 STEP .1
230        GOSUB 360
240     NEXT X
250     FOR X=1 TO 5
260        GOSUB 360
270     NEXT X
280     X=10
290     GOSUB 360
300     X=50
310     GOSUB 360
320     PRINT
330     PRINT
340     PRINT "PROGRAMME ENDS"
350     GOTO 570
360     X0=X*D
370     Y0=M/(4*U)
380     IF X=0 THEN 500
390     IF X<0 THEN 420
400     T=ATN(Y0/X0)
410     GOTO 430
420     T=ATN(Y0/X0)+PI
430     F=U*Y0+M*T/(2*PI)-P
440     F1=U+M*X0/(2*PI*(X0*X0+Y0*Y0))
450     Y0=Y0-F/F1
460     IF ABS(F/F1)<.0001 THEN 480
470     GOTO 390
480     Y=Y0
490     GOTO 510
500     Y=P-Y0
510     U1=U+M*X0/(2*PI*(X0*X0+Y0*Y0))
520     V1=M*Y/(2*PI*(X0*X0+Y0*Y0))
530     Q=SQR(U1*U1+V1*V1)
540     C=1-Q*Q/(U*U)
550     PRINT USING "2X,DDD.DDD,7X,DDD.DDD,4X,DD.DDD,5X,DD.DDD,7X,DD.DDD";X,X0,Y,Q
.C
560     RETURN
570     END
```

```
RUN
PLEASE INPUT THE UNIFORM STREAM SPEED AND THE SOURCE STRENGTH
 5        20
PLEASE INPUT THE STREAM FUNCTION OF THE SELECTED STREAMLINE
IT MUST BE GREATER THAN OR EQUAL TO M/2 WHERE M IS SOURCE STRENGTH
 10

THE STAGNATION POINT IS: D =  .636619772368  METRES UPSTREAM OF THE SOURCE
```

MULTIPLE OF D	X COORD	Y COORD	VELOCITY	PRESSURE COEFFT
-25.000	-15.915	-0.000	4.800	.078
-10.000	-6.366	-0.000	4.500	.190
-5.000	-3.183	-0.000	4.000	.360
-4.000	-2.546	0.000	3.750	.438
-3.000	-1.910	0.000	3.333	.556
-2.000	-1.273	0.000	2.500	.750
-1.500	-.955	0.000	1.667	.889
-1.400	-.891	0.000	1.429	.918
-1.300	-.828	-0.000	1.154	.947
-1.200	-.764	0.000	.833	.972
-1.100	-.700	-0.000	.455	.992
-1.000	-.637	0.000	.001	1.000
-.900	-.573	.345	2.624	.725
-.800	-.509	.483	3.559	.493
-.700	-.446	.586	4.186	.299
-.600	-.382	.670	4.647	.136
-.500	-.318	.742	5.000	-0.000
-.400	-.255	.805	5.277	-.114
-.300	-.191	.861	5.496	-.208
-.200	-.127	.912	5.672	-.287
-.100	-.064	.958	5.814	-.352
0.000	0.000	1.000	5.927	-.405
.100	.064	1.039	6.018	-.449
.200	.127	1.075	6.091	-.484
.300	.191	1.109	6.149	-.512
.400	.255	1.140	6.194	-.535
1.000	.637	1.292	6.298	-.586
2.000	1.273	1.457	6.207	-.541
3.000	1.910	1.563	6.053	-.466
4.000	2.546	1.636	5.912	-.398
5.000	3.183	1.689	5.795	-.343
10.000	6.366	1.822	5.464	-.194
50.000	31.831	1.961	5.100	-.040

```
PROGRAMME ENDS
```

Program notes

(1) Lines 10 to 80 input the source strength and the uniform stream speed and request the operator to select an external streamline by specifying its stream function value; line 70 rejects internal streamlines, and also rejects streamlines in the lower half plane ($y < 0$).

(2) In lines 150 to 310, values of X are specified as multiples of the distance between the source and the stagnation point; these values range from -25 to $+50$ and are more densely packed around the stagnation point where $X = -1$. Statements which calculate the corresponding Y values are placed in a subroutine which commences at line 360.

(3) In the subroutine from 360 to 560, a Newton–Raphson iteration is set up in lines 370 to 480 to solve the equation

$$P = U_y + m/2\pi \arctan (y/x)$$

for y. As in Example 3.1, the correct arctan value must be obtained from the ATN function in lines 390 to 420, and special provision is made for $x = 0$ in 380 and 500. The iteration starting value for y is taken as M/4U in 370. The subroutine concludes with the evaluation of fluid speed and pressure coefficient and prints out the results.

(4) Line 550 exemplifies the PRINT USING statement which permits closer control of both layout and number format than the simple PRINT.

(5) The run shows conditions along the dividing streamline. At a large distance upstream, y is zero and speed and pressure coefficient are nearly at their freestream values of 5 and 0. As the stagnation point is approached, speed reduces to zero (nearly) and C_p rises to $+1$. Downstream of this point, the dividing streamline leaves the x axis, speed initially rises, then falls back towards 5.

Example 3.3   CYLCIRC: cylinder with circulation in a uniform stream

This program calculates surface speeds, pressure coefficients and X and Y component forces on a circular cylinder with circulation. Force coefficients are evaluated by numerical integration of Equations (3.5) and (3.6) and the resulting forces may be compared with the analytical results of Equations (3.22) and (3.23).

```
10      PRINT "PLEASE INPUT THE FREESTREAM SPEED, CYLINDER RADIUS"
20      PRINT "       AND FLUID DENSITY"
30      INPUT U,A,R
40      PRINT U,A,R
50      PRINT
60      PRINT "PLEASE INPUT THE CIRCULATION STRENGTH (ANTICLOCKWISE POSITIVE)"
70      INPUT G
80      PRINT G
90      V=G/(2*PI*A)
100     PRINT
110     PRINT
120     PRINT "Y  FORCE = -DENSITY * SPEED * CIRCULATION = ":-R*U*G
130     PRINT
140     PRINT
150     PRINT "ANGULAR          SURFACE                PRESSURE"
160     PRINT " POSITION         SPEED                COEFFICIENT"
170     PRINT "                (+ ANTICLWSE)"
180     PRINT "--------        --------------        -----------"
190     Sx=0
200     Sy=0
```

```
210     FOR I=0 TO 360 STEP 5
220        T2=I*PI/180
230        V2=-2*U*SIN(T2)+V
240        C2=1-(V2/U)^2
250        IF I/3<>INT(I/3) THEN 270
260        PRINT USING "2X,DDD,14X,DDD.DDD,18X,DDD.DDD";I,V2,C2
270        IF I=0 THEN 300
280        Sx=Sx-(C1+C2)/2*COS((T1+T2)/2)/2
290        Sy=Sy-(C1+C2)/2*SIN((T1+T2)/2)/2
300        T1=T2
310        C1=C2
320     NEXT I
330     X=Sx*5*PI/180
340     Y=Sy*5*PI/180
350     PRINT
360     PRINT
370     PRINT USING """"X FORCE COEFFICIENT = "".DDD.DDD";X
380     PRINT USING """"Y FORCE COEFFICIENT = "".DDD.DDD";Y
390     PRINT
400     PRINT USING """"X FORCE = "",DDDDD.DDD";.5*R*U*U*2*A*X
410     PRINT USING """"Y FORCE = "",DDDDD.DDD";.5*R*U*U*2*A*Y
420     END
```

```
RUN
PLEASE INPUT THE FREESTREAM SPEED, CYLINDER RADIUS
      AND FLUID DENSITY
 5             1          1.225

PLEASE INPUT THE CIRCULATION STRENGTH (ANTICLOCKWISE POSITIVE)
-31.416


Y  FORCE = -DENSITY * SPEED * CIRCULATION =  192.423
```

ANGULAR POSITION	SURFACE SPEED (+ ANTICLWSE)	PRESSURE COEFFICIENT
0	-5.000	-0.000
15	-7.588	-1.303
30	-10.000	-3.000
45	-12.071	-4.828
60	-13.660	-6.464
75	-14.659	-7.596
90	-15.000	-8.000
105	-14.659	-7.596
120	-13.660	-6.464
135	-12.071	-4.828
150	-10.000	-3.000
165	-7.588	-1.303
180	-5.000	-0.000
195	-2.412	.767
210	-0.000	1.000
225	2.071	.828
240	3.660	.464
255	4.659	.132
270	5.000	0.000
285	4.659	.132
300	3.660	.464
315	2.071	.828
330	-0.000	1.000
345	-2.412	.767
360	-5.000	-0.000

```
X FORCE COEFFICIENT =   -0.000
Y FORCE COEFFICIENT =    6.277

X FORCE =     -0.000
Y FORCE =    192.240
```

Program notes

(1) Lines 10 to 120 input data on the flow and print it, together with the theoretical value of the Y force with anticlockwise circulation: $Y = -\rho U\Gamma$ (see Equation (3.23)). Line 90 calculates the surface speed due to the circulation.

(2) Lines 190 and 200 set the numerical summation variables Sx and Sy initially to zero.

(3) From 210 to 320, the program uses a FOR loop to proceed around the cylinder surface in 5° steps, calculating speeds and pressure coefficients; these are printed at 15° intervals. Contributions to the summation variables, Sx and Sy, are added at each step at lines 280 and 290, using mean values of pressure coefficients and angles across each 5° interval. The minus signs preceding the second terms of 280 and 290 are necessary because the integration is proceeding in an anticlockwise direction.

(4) Lines 370 to 410 show how PRINT USING statements may be used to output text as well as control format.

(5) Results of one run are shown, with a circulation giving stagnation points at 210 and 330°, a minimum Cp of −8 at 90° and a 'lift' force of about 192 units per unit cylinder length.

PROBLEMS

(3.1) A two-dimensional flow field is described by the Cartesian velocity components $u = 2y$, $v = 2x$. Write a program which will calculate the velocity and find the position of a fluid particle which lies at point $(-2,3)$ at time $t = 0$, after successive time intervals of $0.01\,\text{s}$. The program is to print out the particle position every $0.1\,\text{s}$ from $t = 0$ to $t = 2$. Then extend the program so that the trajectory printed out is compared with the actual streamline $y^2 - x^2 = 5$.

(3.2) When a source of strength, M, is placed in a freestream, U, at a distance D, directly upstream of an equal strength sink, $-M$, then the dividing streamline is a Rankine oval. Write a program which will print a table of Rankine oval lengths, widths and length/width ratios for the following combinations of source and sink strength, M and separation distance, D. The uniform stream speed is 5.

(a) $D = 1$ and M ranges from 10 to 1 in steps of 1.
(b) $M = 10$ and D ranges from 2 to 0.2 in steps of 0.2, then from 0.2 to 0.02 in steps of 0.02.

(c) D ranges from 2 to 0.05 in steps of 0.05 while M simultaneously changes from 10 to 400 so that the product MD remains constant at 20.

Note that in (a), the width of the oval decreases towards zero as M decreases; in (b), both length and width decrease towards zero as D decreases; but in (c), both length and width remain finite with their ratio tending to 1, i.e. as the source-sink pair tends to a doublet, the dividing streamline tends to a circle.

(3.3) Write a program, similar to Example 3.2, which calculates coordinates of points along a selected streamline in the flow of a uniform stream around a cylinder with circulation.

(3.4) The pressure distribution on the surface of a real cylinder may be approximately represented by Equation (3.21): $C_p = 1 - 4\sin^2\theta$ from the forward stagnation point round to the point on the downstream side where separation occurs and thereafter C_p remains constant. Separation may be considered to occur where, in ideal flow, the pressure gradient $dC_p/d\theta$ is equal to $+3.0$. Write a program which will input the cylinder radius and the freestream speed, calculate cylinder surface conditions at $1°$ intervals and print out, at $5°$ intervals, the pressure coefficient and the pressure gradient (calculated numerically), together with the value of the overall drag coefficient.

(3,5) Write a program which calculates numerically the values at (10.10) of the stream function (Equation (3.7)) and the potential function (Equation (3.8)) for the two flows:

(a) $u = 10y$, $v = 10x$ which is irrotational
(b) $u = 10y$, v $= 0$ which is rotational

Choose two different integration paths so that it can be seen that ψ does not depend upon integration path for either flow, but that ϕ is independent of path only for flow (a).

(3.6) Write a program which will input the coordinates (X, Y) of the centre and radius (R) of a circle and calculate, by numerical integration of Equation (3.11), the circulation around the circle circumference in the free vortex flow given by $q_\theta = 100/2\pi r$. By inputting suitable values of X, Y and R, show that the circulation is 100 or 0 depending on whether the origin is inside or outside the circle. Then, modify the program to change the flow to a forced vortex $q_\theta = 100r$ and it will now be found that the circulation depends only on the area of the circle.

Chapter 4

Boundary layers

ESSENTIAL THEORY

4.1 Introduction and qualitative description

The particles of a moving fluid adjacent to a solid surface are
stationary relative to the surface (the no slip condition) and, at
high Reynolds numbers, it is observed that, at a small distance
from the surface, fluid moves with a velocity which is comparable
with free stream. There is, therefore, a thin layer close to the
surface in which fluid strains (velocity gradients) are large and,
because all real fluids are viscous, large viscous stresses are
generated. This layer is called the *boundary layer*. Outside this
layer, velocity gradients are small and inviscid fluid theories may
be applied.

4.1.1 Boundary layer description

The general characteristics of the boundary layer are shown in
Figure 4.1.

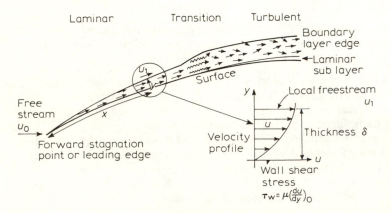

Figure 4.1 Boundary layer characteristics

46

From the leading edge, or forward stagnation point, the boundary layer is initially laminar with momentum transport across the layer occurring on a molecular scale only; the shear stresses, τ, are governed by

$$\tau = \mu \frac{\partial u}{\partial y} \qquad (4.1)$$

The laminar boundary layer develops instabilities as local Reynolds number based on distance, x, from the leading edge increases and a transition region, where there is a marked increase in boundary layer thickness, is followed by a turbulent boundary layer. In the turbulent layer, macroscopic mixing occurs, resulting in large-scale transfer of momentum across the layer and effectively introducing additional stresses called Reynolds stresses.

Velocity profiles

Velocity profiles for the laminar and turbulent layers are significantly different as shown in Figure 4.2. Except near the laminar boundary layer leading edge, laminar surface friction stresses are generally less than turbulent surface friction stresses.

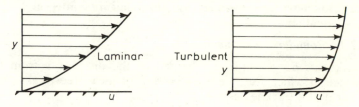

Figure 4.2 Laminar and turbulent boundary layer velocity profiles

Effects of a pressure gradient

A pressure gradient will exert a powerful influence on boundary layer growth and velocity profile. A positive pressure gradient will advance transition and, if sufficiently strong, may cause separation.

4.1.2   Boundary layer separation

Under the action of an increasing positive (adverse) pressure gradient, the surface velocity gradient, $\partial u/\partial y$, decreases to zero and then to a negative value; at zero, the boundary layer separates from the surface. Separation leads to a large diameter wake. Other conditions being equal, a laminar boundary layer is much more likely to separate than a turbulent layer because the large-scale mixing in the turbulent layer provides a mechanism for re-energizing the inner regions close to the surface.

4.1.3 Boundary layer drag

Boundary layer drag consists of two components:

(1) *Surface friction drag* resulting from the total effect of the friction shear forces over the surface of the body.

(2) *Normal pressure drag* resulting from the total effect of the pressure forces over the surface of the body. In inviscid flow, d'Alembert's paradox states that the pressure drag force on a closed body is zero, but the boundary layer and wake modify the effective body shape, and the changes in streamline pattern, velocities and pressures produce a non-zero pressure force. The closer a real flow is to an inviscid flow, the smaller the pressure drag; conversely, separation results in large pressure drag forces.

4.2   Boundary layer thickness and the momentum integral equation

4.2.1 Boundary layer thickness

Thickness, δ, is arbitrarily defined as the distance y from the surface at which fluid velocity is 99% of local freestream. Two other useful thicknesses are

$$\delta^* = \int_0^\delta \left(1 - \frac{u}{U_1}\right) dy \tag{4.2}$$

This is called the *displacement thickness* because it represents the distance the surface would have to be displaced in the y direction to reduce the volume flow by an amount equal to the actual reduction due to the boundary layer; it also indicates the amount a streamline is displaced by the boundary layer flow retardation.

$$\theta = \int_0^\delta \frac{u}{U_1}\left(1 - \frac{u}{U_1}\right) dy \tag{4.3}$$

This is called the *momentum thickness* because it represents the distance the surface would have to be displaced to reduce the momentum flow by an amount equal to the actual reduction due to the boundary layer.

The rate at which boundary layer thickness grows is related to the wall (surface) shear stress τ_w by the momentum integral equation which for incompressible steady flow is

$$\tau_w = \rho \frac{\partial}{\partial x} (U_1^2 \theta) + \rho U_1 \frac{\partial U_1}{\partial x} \delta^* \qquad (4.4)$$

In non-dimensional form, it is

$$\frac{c_f}{2} = \frac{\partial \theta}{\partial x} + \frac{\partial U_1}{\partial x} \frac{\theta}{U_1} (2 + H) \qquad (4.5)$$

where $c_f = \tau_w / \frac{1}{2} \rho U_1^2$ is the local skin friction coefficient and $H = \delta^*/\theta$ is the boundary layer shape factor.

4.3 Laminar boundary layer theory

The steady incompressible form of the Navier–Stokes equations in two dimensions may be simplified for a thin boundary layer to the *boundary layer equations*

$$u \frac{\partial u}{\partial x} + v \frac{\partial u}{\partial y} = \frac{1}{\rho} \frac{\partial p}{\partial x} + \nu \frac{\partial^2 u}{\partial y^2} \qquad (4.7)$$

$$\frac{\partial p}{\partial y} = 0 \qquad (4.8)$$

and the continuity equation is

$$\frac{\partial u}{\partial x} + \frac{\partial v}{\partial y} = 0 \qquad (4.9)$$

Equation (4.8) shows that pressure is constant across the boundary layer.

4.3.1 *Zero pressure gradient*

For a flat plate at zero incidence, pressure is constant, and if the coordinate transformation defined by

$$\eta = \frac{y}{2} \left(\frac{U_1}{\nu x} \right)^{1/2} \qquad (4.10)$$

is introduced, the boundary layer equations reduce to the Blasius equation

$$ff'' + f''' = 0 \tag{4.11}$$

where f is defined by Equation (4.12) below and dashes denote derivatives with respect to η. The boundary conditions are: $f = f' = 0$ at $\eta = 0$, and $f' = 2$ at $\eta = \infty$. The solution of Equation (4.11) leads to

$$u = U_1 f'/2 \tag{4.12}$$

$$v = (U_1 v/x)^{1/2} (\eta f' - f)/2 \tag{4.13}$$

$$c_f = 0.664/\mathrm{Re}_x^{1/2} \tag{4.14}$$

$$\delta^*/x = 1.729/\mathrm{Re}_x^{1/2} \tag{4.15}$$

$$\theta/x = 0.664/\mathrm{Re}_x^{1/2} \tag{4.16}$$

4.3.2   Non-zero pressure gradient

If there is a pressure gradient in the flow external to the boundary layer such that the external velocity U_1 is described by $U_1 = Kx^m$, then the boundary layer equations reduce to the Falkner–Skan equation:

$$f''' + (m + 1)ff'' - 2mf'^2 + 8m = 0 \tag{4.17}$$

where dashes denote derivatives with respect to η, defined by Equation (4.10). The solution leads to

$$u = U_1 f'/2 \tag{4.18}$$

$$v = -(U_1 v/x)^{1/2}\{(m + 1)f + (m - 1)\eta f'\}/2 \tag{4.19}$$

Boundary conditions are the same as for Equation (4.11). The boundary layer in the neighbourhood of a stagnation point is represented by $m = 1$, and at a separation point by $m = -0.0904$. Skin friction coefficient is given by

$$c_f = F(m)/\mathrm{Re}_x^{1/2} \tag{4.20}$$

where $F(-0.0904) = 0$, $F(0) = 0.664$ (Blasius) and $F(1) = 2.466$.

4.3.3   Pohlhausen's method

If it is assumed that the boundary layer velocity profile in the presence of an external pressure gradient can be described by a quartic algebraic relation between u/U_1 and $y/\delta = \eta$, then

$$u/U_1 = 2\eta - 2\eta^3 + \eta^4 + \lambda\eta(1 - \eta)^3/6 \tag{4.21}$$

where

$$\lambda = \delta^2/\nu \cdot dU_1/dx \qquad (4.22)$$

Separation corresponds to $\lambda = -12$ and a stagnation point to $\lambda = 7.052$, and:

$$c_f = 4\nu \left(1 + \frac{\lambda}{12}\right)/U_1\delta \qquad (4.23)$$

Boundary layer thickness is obtained, for prescribed $U_1(x)$, from a solution of the momentum integral Equation (4.4) (see Example 4.4).

4.4 Transition

Disturbances in the laminar boundary layer are damped by viscosity at low values of local Reynolds number (Re_x) but at high Re_x they are amplified, and develop, first into spots of turbulence, and then into fully turbulent conditions in the boundary layer; the range of critical transition Reynolds numbers extends from 10^5 to 2×10^6. Factors which tend to cause earlier transitions are freestream turbulence, noise, surface roughness, high surface temperature, an adverse pressure gradient and a low Mach number. A transition which commences at a lower value of Re_x extends over a finite streamwise distance but for Re_x of the order of 10^6 and above; this region is sufficiently small to be considered a point – the transition point. For general engineering calculations, transition may be taken to occur on a smooth flat plate at a local Reynolds number of 5×10^5 as long as the external flow is reasonably turbulence free.

4.5 Turbulent boundary layers

If the instantaneous velocity components at a point in a turbulent flow are written $(\bar{u} + u)$, $(\bar{v} + v)$ where u and v are deviations from time averages $(\bar{u}, \bar{v})$, then the Reynolds stresses referred to in Section 4.1 may be expressed $-\rho\overline{uv}$ where the bar denotes the time average value. The total shear stress acting in a turbulent boundary layer is therefore

$$\tau = \mu \frac{\partial \bar{u}}{\partial y} - \rho\overline{uv} \qquad (4.24)$$

Compared with the laminar boundary layer case, the $\overline{uv}$ term is an additional variable in the equations governing the turbulent flow.

Great difficulty has been experienced in satisfactorily relating this quantity to the other flow variables and consequently the set of turbulent boundary layer equations is not properly formulated.

Equation (4.24) holds for the inner regions of the turbulent layer. Very close to the surface, the velocity fluctuations are constrained by the presence of the wall and the Reynolds stress term becomes small compared with the $\mu \partial u / \partial y$ term. Further out, the flow is fully turbulent and the Reynolds stress term dominates. In the outer regions, the turbulence is intermittent and Equation (4.24) does not apply, but this region may be described by modified forms of the equations developed for the fully turbulent region.

4.5.1   Mixing length theory

Turbulence may be treated as being analogous to the random motion of the molecules of a gas. If a mixing length ℓ is postulated over which an eddy is assumed to retain its random velocity before mixing with the surrounding fluid, then Equation (4.24) may be written:

$$\tau = \left(\mu + \rho \ell^2 \left| \frac{\partial u}{\partial y} \right| \right) \frac{\partial u}{\partial y} \qquad (4.25)$$

For the fully turbulent region, the first term may be neglected and, if it is assumed that ℓ is proportional to distance from the surface y, then Equation (4.25) may be integrated to

$$u/u_\tau = A \log_{10} (y u_\tau / \nu) + B \qquad (4.26)$$

where $u_\tau = (\tau_w / \rho)^{1/2}$ is the friction velocity and A and B have been determined experimentally to be 5.75 and 5.5 respectively. Equation (4.26) is known as the log law but it cannot apply to very small values of y, i.e. close to the wall.

4.5.2   Inner velocity law

In the laminar sub-layer, Reynolds stresses are negligible and it may be assumed that the stress, now expressed by $\tau_w = \mu \partial u / \partial y$, is constant across the sublayer. Integrating gives

$$u/u_\tau = y u_\tau / \nu \qquad (4.27)$$

Outer regions

At the outer edges of the turbulent layer, intermittency of the turbulence is appreciable and the log law (4.26) is modified to

$$u/u_\tau = 1/k \cdot \log_{10}(yu_\tau/v) + \phi(y/\delta) \qquad (4.28)$$

which covers both the fully turbulent region where $\phi = $ const. $= B$, and the outer layers. Since $u = U_1$ at $y = \delta$, then

$$(U_1 - u)/u_\tau = \phi(1) - 1/k \cdot \log_{10}(y/\delta) - \phi(y/\delta) = f(y/\delta) \qquad (4.29)$$

where $\phi(1)$ is a universal constant, f and ϕ are found experimentally; $\phi(1)$ has been measured as 7.90 and k as 0.4. f and ϕ depend strongly on external pressure gradient.

4.5.3   Skin friction and flat plate drag coefficient

Using the velocity laws described above and experimental results, von Karman derived the equation

$$c_f^{-1/2} = 1.7 + 4.15 \log_{10}(\mathrm{Re}_x c_f) \qquad (4.30)$$

to relate the local friction coefficient with the local Reynolds number; and the equation

$$C_f^{-1/2} = 4.13 \log_{10}(\mathrm{Re}_L C_f) \qquad (4.31)$$

to relate flat plate friction drag coefficient (one side) with plate Reynolds number assuming that the whole plate is covered by a turbulent boundary layer. Schlichting fitting the following interpolation formulae to results obtained by Prandtl

$$c_f = (2 \log_{10} \mathrm{Re}_x - 0.65)^{-2.3} \qquad (4.32)$$

$$C_f = 0.455 (\log_{10} \mathrm{Re}_L)^{-2.58} \qquad (4.33)$$

for $10^5 < \mathrm{Re}_L < 1.5 \times 10^9$ and the boundary layer all turbulent.

Power laws

Experimental results show that the 'power law'

$$u/U_1 = (y/\delta)^{1/n} \qquad (4.34)$$

is a good interpolation formula for the turbulent boundary layer velocity profile except close to the wall. n lies between 5 and 9 depending on Reynolds number. Displacement and momentum thicknesses are:

$$\delta^*/\delta = 1/(n+1) \qquad (4.35)$$

and

$$\theta/\delta = n/(n + 1)(n + 2) \qquad (4.36)$$

For $5 \times 10^5 < Re_x < 10^7$, n may be taken to be 7 and, using this value together with a friction factor/Reynolds number correlation for pipe flow, it may be shown that

$$\delta/x = 0.370/Re_x^{1/5} \qquad (4.37)$$

$$c_f = 0.059/Re_x^{1/5} = 0.026/Re_\theta^{1/4} \qquad (4.38)$$

$$C_f = 0.074/Re_L^{1/5} \qquad (4.39)$$

For $10^6 < Re_x < 10^8$, a good fit is provided by $n = 9$, giving

$$\delta/x = 0.275/Re_x^{1/6} \qquad (4.40)$$

$$c_f = 0.038/Re_x^{1/6} = 0.018\,Re_\theta^{1/5} \qquad (4.41)$$

$$C_f = 0.045/Re_L^{1/6} \qquad (4.42)$$

4.5.4   Non-zero external pressure gradient

If the boundary layer velocity profile may be approximated by a power law equation with an appropriate value of n, then H may be calculated from Equations (4.35) and (4.36), and c_f may be expressed in terms of θ using Equation (4.38) or (4.41). The momentum integral Equation (4.5) can now be solved for θ, either analytically if U_1 is of suitable form, or numerically.

WORKED EXAMPLES

Example 4.1   TRANSTRIP: positioning of wind tunnel transition strip

As discussed in Chapter 2, attempts to reproduce flow conditions around a full-scale vehicle by means of a wind or water tunnel model test cannot be fully successful unless the model and full-scale Reynolds numbers are the same. This equality is very difficult to achieve in practice in an unpressurized wind tunnel. In particular, the boundary layer transition point will not be properly positioned on the model so that measurements of skin friction drag may be in error by a significant amount. However, this error may be partially corrected by placing a 'transition strip' on the model to promote transition at the correct point. The strip may take the form of a wire stretched spanwise along the surface or a band of rough surface material glued to the surface.

This program inputs the chord of a full-scale aircraft wing and the standard atmosphere altitude at which it is intended to operate; it will then input the model chord length and, assuming that a wind tunnel test is being conducted at sea level conditions, output the Reynolds numbers and the chordwise station at which a transition strip should be fixed on the model for correct representation of the full-scale transition position.

```
10    PRINT "PLEASE INPUT THE CHORD, SPEED AND ALTITUDE OF THE FULL SCALE AIRCRA
FT"
20    INPUT Ca,Ua,H
30    PRINT Ca,Ua,H
40    PRINT
50    PRINT "PLEASE INPUT THE MODEL CHORD AND TUNNEL SPEED   ";
60    INPUT Cm,Um
70    PRINT Cm,Um
80    PRINT
90    IF H>11000 THEN 130
100     T=288-.0065*H
110     D=1.225*(T/288)^4.259
120   GOTO 150
130     T=216.5
140     D=.3648*EXP((11000-H)/6334)
150   Mu=.000001458*T^1.5/(T+110.4)
160   Ra=D*Ua*Ca/Mu
170   PRINT "FULL SCALE REYNOLDS NUMBER = ";Ra
180   PRINT "MODEL REYNOLDS NUMBER = ";1.225*Um*Cm/.000017894
190   PRINT
200   PRINT "FULL SCALE TRANSITION OCCURS AT ";50000000/Ra;" PER CENT CHORD"
210   PRINT "REQUIRED TRANSITION STRIP POSITION IS AT ";500000/Ra*Cm;" M"
220   END
```

```
RUN
PLEASE INPUT THE CHORD, SPEED AND ALTITUDE OF THE FULL SCALE AIRCRAFT
  2        150        10000

PLEASE INPUT THE MODEL CHORD AND TUNNEL SPEED   .4        80

FULL SCALE REYNOLDS NUMBER = 8.48957455655E+6
MODEL REYNOLDS NUMBER = 2.1906784397E+6

FULL SCALE TRANSITION OCCURS AT 5.88957664097  PER CENT CHORD
REQUIRED TRANSITION STRIP POSITION IS AT .0235583065639  M


RUN
PLEASE INPUT THE CHORD, SPEED AND ALTITUDE OF THE FULL SCALE AIRCRAFT
  3        200        0

PLEASE INPUT THE MODEL CHORD AND TUNNEL SPEED   .6        100

FULL SCALE REYNOLDS NUMBER = 4.10922965119E+7
MODEL REYNOLDS NUMBER = 4.10752207444E+6

FULL SCALE TRANSITION OCCURS AT 1.21677307535  PER CENT CHORD
REQUIRED TRANSITION STRIP POSITION IS AT .00730063845211  M
```

Program notes

(1) Lines 10 to 70 input the full-scale aircraft and model test data.

(2) Lines 90 to 150 calculate air temperature, density and viscosity at the specified altitude using the atmosphere equations and Sutherland's formula introduced in Chapter 2.

(3) Lines 160 to 180 calculate and print the full-scale and test Reynolds numbers, and lines 210 and 220 calculate and print transition point information based on a transition Reynolds number of 500 000.

Example 4.2   BOUNCALC: the reduction of experimental measurements of a boundary layer velocity profile

The analysis of boundary layer profile measurements generates a considerable amount of arithmetical work in the course of calculating boundary layer thicknesses, comparing with theoretical results and finding best straight line fits. Computer assistance is appropriate for this work and the following program contains some of the reduction procedures appropriate to boundary layer experiments. The program takes in, as a DATA statement, measured values of dynamic pressure (mm water) sensed by a very fine forward facing pitot tube as it is traversed across the boundary layer some distance from the leading edge of a flat plate at zero incidence in a 15 m/s (U_0) airflow.

Distance from surface y (m)	Pressure p (mm water)	Distance from surface y (m)	Pressure p (mm water)
0	0	0.011	11.95
0.001	5.35	0.012	12.26
0.002	7.01	0.013	12.51
0.003	8.08	0.014	12.80
0.004	8.87	0.015	13.06
0.005	9.53	0.016	13.31
0.006	10.04	0.017	13.53
0.007	10.45	0.018	13.77
0.008	10.88	0.019	13.99
0.009	11.27	0.020	14.05
0.010	11.62		

An initial inspection of the variation of velocity, u, with distance, y, from the plate surface indicates that the boundary layer is turbulent with a thickness, δ, of 0.018 m. The program then tabulates the following quantities at the measured distances, y: measured pressure, p, velocity, u, $z = y/\delta$, $v = u/U_0$, $z^{1/7}$, $\log_{10} y$, $\ln z$, $\ln v$; appropriate graphs may then be plotted manually from these values if required.

Also calculated are boundary layer thicknesses δ^* and θ, using the trapezoidal rule to perform the necessary integration; the apparent distance, x, from the plate leading edge is derived from Equation (4.37) and theoretical values of local skin friction coefficient c_f are found from this distance. Using a best straight line fit to values of $\ln(y/\delta)$ and $\ln(u/U_0)$, the most suitable value of n in Equation (4.34) is found. Further discussion of the results is included in the program notes.

```
!0      OPTION BASE 1
20      DIM Y(21),P(21),Z(21),U(21),V(21),Lgy(21),Lnz(21),Lnv(21)
30      D=1.225
40      Nu=.000014607
50      U0=15
60      Del=.018
70      DATA 0,0,.001,5.35,.002,7.01,.003,8.08,.004,8.87,.005,9.53,.006,10.04
80      DATA .007,10.45,.008,10.88,.009,11.27,.010,11.62,.011,11.95,.012,12.26
90      DATA .013,12.51,.014,12.80,.015,13.06,.016,13.31,.017,13.53,.018,13.77
100     DATA .019,13.99,.020,14.05
110     PRINT "     Y          P          U      Z=Y/DEL   V=U/U0    Z^1/7     LG Y      LN Z      L
N V"
120     PRINT "    (M)     (MM H2O)   (M/S)"
130     PRINT
140         Sdst=0
150         Sth=0
160          Sz=0
170          Sv=0
180          Szv=0
190          Szz=0
200     FOR I=1 TO 21
210         READ Y(I),P(I)
220         Z(I)=Y(I)/Del
230         U(I)=SQR(2*9.81*P(I)/1.225)
240         V(I)=U(I)/U0
250         IF I=1 THEN 360
260             Sdst=Sdst+(1-V(I-1)+1-V(I))/2
270             Sth=Sth+(V(I-1)*(1-V(I-1))+V(I)*(1-V(I)))/2
280             Lgy(I)=LOG(Y(I))/2.303
290             Lnz(I)=LOG(Z(I))
300             Lnv(I)=LOG(V(I))
310             Sz=Sz+Lnz(I)
320             Sv=Sv+Lnv(I)
330             Szv=Szv+Lnz(I)*Lnv(I)
340             Szz=Szz+Lnz(I)*Lnz(I)
350             GOTO 390
360             Lgy(1)=0
370             Lnz(1)=0
380             Lnv(1)=0
390         PRINT USING "DD.DDD,2X";Y(I),P(I),U(I),Z(I),V(I),(Z(I))^(1/7),Lgy(I),Lnz
(I),Lnv(I)
400     NEXT I
410     N=1/((20*Szv-Sz*Sv)/(20*Szz-Sz*Sz))
420     PRINT
430     PRINT "CALCULATED N = ";N
440     PRINT "                                            EQNS (4.35) & (4.
36)"
450     PRINT "                             MEASURED        N=7        CALCULA
TED N"
460     PRINT USING "31A,3(.DDDDD,10X)";"DISPLACEMENT THICKNESS (M) = ";Sdst*.001;
Del/8;Del/(N+1)
470     PRINT USING "31A,3(.DDDDD,10X)";"MOMENTUM THICKNESS (M) = ";Sth*.001;Del*7
/72;Del*N/(N+1)/(N+2)
480     PRINT USING "30A,3(D.DDD,11X)";"SHAPE FACTOR, H = ";Sdst/Sth;9/7;(N+2)/N
490     PRINT
500     X=(Del/.37)^1.25*(U0/Nu)^.25
510     PRINT "APPARENT DISTANCE FROM THE LEADING EDGE = ";X;" M"
520     Rex=U0*X/Nu
530     PRINT "APPARENT LOCAL REYNOLDS NUMBER = ";Rex
540     PRINT
550     PRINT "USING EQUATION (4.38):"
560     PRINT "LOCAL SKIN FRICTION COEFFICIENT = ";.059/(Rex^.2)
570     PRINT
580     PRINT "USING EQUATION (4.32):"
590     PRINT "LOCAL SKIN FRICTION COEFFICIENT = ";(2*LOG(Rex)/2.303-.65)^(-2.3)
600     END
```

```
RUN
     Y         P        U     Z=Y/DEL  V=U/U0   Z 1/7    LG Y     LN Z     LN V
    (M)    (MM H2O)  (M/S)

  0.000    0.000    0.000    0.000    0.000    0.000    0.000    0.000    0.000
   .001    5.350    9.257     .056     .617     .662   -2.999   -2.890    -.483
   .002    7.010   10.596     .111     .706     .731   -2.698   -2.197    -.348
   .003    8.080   11.376     .167     .758     .774   -2.522   -1.792    -.277
   .004    8.870   11.919     .222     .795     .807   -2.398   -1.504    -.230
   .005    9.530   12.355     .278     .824     .833   -2.301   -1.281    -.194
   .006   10.040   12.681     .333     .845     .855   -2.221   -1.099    -.168
   .007   10.450   12.937     .389     .862     .874   -2.155    -.944    -.148
   .008   10.880   13.201     .444     .880     .891   -2.097    -.811    -.128
   .009   11.270   13.435     .500     .896     .906   -2.045    -.693    -.110
   .010   11.620   13.642     .556     .909     .919   -2.000    -.588    -.095
   .011   11.950   13.835     .611     .922     .932   -1.958    -.492    -.081
   .012   12.260   14.013     .667     .934     .944   -1.920    -.405    -.068
   .013   12.510   14.155     .722     .944     .955   -1.886    -.325    -.058
   .014   12.800   14.318     .778     .955     .965   -1.854    -.251    -.047
   .015   13.060   14.463     .833     .964     .974   -1.824    -.182    -.036
   .016   13.310   14.601     .889     .973     .983   -1.796    -.118    -.027
   .017   13.530   14.721     .944     .981     .992   -1.769    -.057    -.019
   .018   13.770   14.851    1.000     .990    1.000   -1.744    0.000    -.010
   .019   13.990   14.969    1.056     .998    1.008   -1.721     .054    -.002
   .020   14.050   15.001    1.111    1.000    1.015   -1.699     .105    0.000

CALCULATED N =   6.3946968787

                                                         EQNS (4.35) & (4.36)
                                     MEASURED         N=7           CALCULATED N
DISPLACEMENT THICKNESS (M) =          .00275          .00225             .00243
MOMENTUM THICKNESS (M) =              .00179          .00175             .00185
SHAPE FACTOR, H =                    1.537           1.286              1.313

APPARENT DISTANCE FROM THE LEADING EDGE =   .727312469988   M
APPARENT LOCAL REYNOLDS NUMBER =   746880.745521

USING EQUATION (4.38):
LOCAL SKIN FRICTION COEFFICIENT =   .0039464059654

USING EQUATION (4.32):
LOCAL SKIN FRICTION COEFFICIENT =   .00394695748977
```

Program notes

(1) The OPTION BASE statement is required by some computers to define the default lower bound of arrays (in this case, arrays elements start at 1); on other machines, it may not be necessary to include this statement.

(2) Lines 30 to 100 input freestream and boundary layer parameters; the DATA statements carry the measured values of Y and P.

(3) Lines 140 and 150 set to zero the initial values of Sdst and Sth which accumulate the sums required for finding boundary layer thicknesses, δ^* and θ, by numerical integration. Lines 160 to 190 set to zero the initial values of Sz, Sv, Szv and Szz which accumulate the sums required for calculating the best straight line fit to values of $\ln(U/U0)$ and $\ln(Y/\delta)$; they accumulate $\ln(Y/\delta)$, $\ln(U/U0)$, their product and the square of $\ln(Y/\delta)$ respectively.

(4) The FOR loop from 200 to 400 reads data (210), calculates velocities and appropriate functions (220 to 240 and 280 to 300),

accumulates integration sums using the trapezoidal rule (260 and 270), accumulates regression sums (310 to 340) and prints results (390).

At the plate surface where Y and U are zero, log values cannot be calculated and, in order not to complicate the printing of results unduly, the log values have been artificially set at zero by statements 250 and 360 to 380.

(5) The PRINT USING statement at 390 controls output layout.

(6) Line 410 calculates the best value for N, the index relating Y/δ and U/U0 of Equation (4.34); this is printed at 430. After printing suitable headings at lines 440 and 450, lines 460 to 480 tabulate boundary layer thicknesses and shape factor, as measured and as predicted by Equations (4.35) and (4.36) with N = 7 and with N equal to the calculated value. More PRINT USING statements control table layout.

(7) Line 500 calculates the apparent distance (X) from the plate leading edge to the traverse point, based on the assumption that the boundary layer is turbulent from the leading edge and that Equation (4.37) is therefore valid; this equation, however, assumes N = 7. Using this value of X, local Reynolds number is evaluated and then inserted into Equations (4.32) and (4.38) to find the local skin friction factor (c_f); the values given by these two independent 'semi-empirical' equations happen to agree remarkably well.

(8) The program RUN gives the processed data calculated from the input values. Column 5 may be compared with column 6 in order to assess the validity of the one-seventh power law. The value of the index N is found to be less than 7 which is probably correct for the low value of Reynolds number. Boundary layer thicknesses agree moderately well.

Example 4.3   PLATEDRAG: the investigation of conditions in a flat plate boundary layer which is partly laminar and partly turbulent

To calculate skin friction drag and other parameters on a flat plate over which the boundary layer changes from laminar to turbulent, it is necessary to know the position of the transition point and it is also necessary to know what changes in boundary layer properties occur at transition. The assumption that is normally made is that the momentum thickness remains unchanged, with consequent discontinuities in the other thicknesses. If the transition point is specified, then the apparent origin of the turbulent boundary layer may be found and its momentum thickness at the plate trailing edge may be calculated. As this thickness is, by definition, a measure of the momentum deficit in the boundary layer fluid, it will be related to the friction drag on the plate. This program inputs freestream fluid properties, flat plate length and transition point position. It outputs drag and drag coefficient, together with laminar and turbulent boundary layer and transition point parameters.

```
10      PRINT "PLEASE INPUT FREESTREAM SPEED, DENSITY AND VISCOSITY ";
20      INPUT U,Ro,Mu
30      PRINT U,Ro,Mu
40      Nu=Mu/Ro
50      PRINT
60      PRINT "PLEASE INPUT THE PLATE LENGTH ";
70      INPUT C
80      PRINT C
90      PRINT
100     PRINT "DO YOU WISH TO SPECIFY:"
110     PRINT "            1.  |TRANSITION POINT DISTANCE FROM THE LEADING EDGE"
120     PRINT "            2.   TRANSITION POINT REYNOLDS NUMBER"
130     PRINT "ANSWER 1 OR 2 ":
140     INPUT Z
150     PRINT Z
160     IF Z<>1 AND Z<>2 THEN 100
170     PRINT
180     IF Z=2 THEN 240
190     PRINT "PLEASE GIVE TRANSITION POINT DISTANCE ";
200     INPUT Xt
210     PRINT Xt
220     Rt=U*Xt/Nu
230     GOTO 280
240     PRINT "PLEASE GIVE TRANSITION REYNOLDS NUMBER ";
250     INPUT Rt
260     PRINT Rt
270     Xt=Rt*Nu/U
280     PRINT
290     IF Xt=0 THEN 330
300     Dtl=4.91*Xt/SQR(Rt)
310     Th=.664*Xt/SQR(Rt)
320     GOTO 350
330     Dtl=0
340     Th=0
350     Dtt=Th*72/7
360     X1=(Dtt/.37)`1.25*(U/Nu)`.25
370     Xte=C-Xt+X1
380     Thte=7/72*.37*Xte/(U*Xte/Nu)`(.2)
390     D=Ro*U*U*Thte
400     Cd=2*Thte/C
410     PRINT "TRANSITION DISTANCE = ";Xt
420     PRINT "TRANSITION REYNOLDS NUMBER = ";Rt
430     PRINT
440     PRINT "TRANSITION MOMENTUM THICKNESS = ";Th
450     PRINT "LAMINAR B L THICKNESS AT TRANSITION = ";Dtl
460     PRINT "TURBULENT B L THICKNESS AT TRANSITION = ";Dtt
470     PRINT "DISTANCE FROM TURBULENT B L APPARENT ORIGIN TO TRANSITION = ";X1
480     PRINT
490     PRINT "MOMENTUM THICKNESS AT TRAILING EDGE = ";Thte
500     PRINT "PLATE TOTAL DRAG = ";D
510     PRINT "LAMINAR B L DRAG = ";Ro*U*U*Th
520     PRINT "TURBULENT B L DRAG = ";D-Ro*U*U*Th
530     PRINT
540     PRINT "PLATE DRAG COEFFICIENT = ";Cd
550     PRINT "PLATE REYNOLDS NUMBER = ";U*C/Nu
560     END
```

```
RUN
PLEASE INPUT FREESTREAM SPEED, DENSITY AND VISCOSITY  15      1.225      1.789E-5

PLEASE INPUT THE PLATE LENGTH  1

DO YOU WISH TO SPECIFY:
           1.    TRANSITION POINT DISTANCE FROM THE LEADING EDGE
           2.    TRANSITION POINT REYNOLDS NUMBER
ANSWER 1 OR 2  1

PLEASE GIVE TRANSITION POINT DISTANCE  1

TRANSITION DISTANCE = 1
TRANSITION REYNOLDS NUMBER = 1.02711011738E+6

TRANSITION MOMENTUM THICKNESS = .000655178407027
LAMINAR B L THICKNESS AT TRANSITION = .00484476803991
TURBULENT B L THICKNESS AT TRANSITION = .00673897790085
DISTANCE FROM TURBULENT B L APPARENT ORIGIN TO TRANSITION = .213007373323

MOMENTUM THICKNESS AT TRAILING EDGE = .000655178407027
PLATE TOTAL DRAG = .180583548437
LAMINAR B L DRAG = .180583548437
TURBULENT B L DRAG = -2.77555756156E-17

PLATE DRAG COEFFICIENT = .00131035681405
PLATE REYNOLDS NUMBER = 1.02711011738E+6


RUN
PLEASE INPUT FREESTREAM SPEED, DENSITY AND VISCOSITY  80      1.225      1.789E-5

PLEASE INPUT THE PLATE LENGTH  10

DO YOU WISH TO SPECIFY:
           1.    TRANSITION POINT DISTANCE FROM THE LEADING EDGE
           2.    TRANSITION POINT REYNOLDS NUMBER
ANSWER 1 OR 2  2

PLEASE GIVE TRANSITION REYNOLDS NUMBER  500000

TRANSITION DISTANCE = .0912755102041
TRANSITION REYNOLDS NUMBER = 500000

TRANSITION MOMENTUM THICKNESS = 8.57111547902E-5
LAMINAR B L THICKNESS AT TRANSITION = .000633797846416
TURBULENT B L THICKNESS AT TRANSITION = .000881600449271
DISTANCE FROM TURBULENT B L APPARENT ORIGIN TO TRANSITION = .025467805956

MOMENTUM THICKNESS AT TRAILING EDGE = .0101379505963
PLATE TOTAL DRAG = 79.4815326752
LAMINAR B L DRAG = .671975453555
TURBULENT B L DRAG = 78.8095572216

PLATE DRAG COEFFICIENT = .00202759011926
PLATE REYNOLDS NUMBER = 5.47792062605E+7
```

Program notes

(1) Lines 100 to 270 allow the operator to supply values of either transition distance or transition Reynolds number.

(2) Lines 300 and 310 calculate the 99% thickness, Dtl, of the laminar layer and the momentum thickness, Th, at the transition point, using two equations of Blasius laminar boundary layer theory. Special provision (lines 290, 330 and 340) is made for the case where transition occurs at the leading edge ($Xt = Rt = 0$).

(3) Line 350 calculates the thickness of the turbulent layer, Dtt, at the transition point assuming that the momentum thickness is

unchanged. Line 360 finds the distance (X1) of the apparent origin
of the turbulent layer upstream of transition and then line 370
calculates the distance, Xte, of the plate trailing edge from this
point. This allows calculation of the momentum thickness at the
trailing edge, Thte, in line 380 from which drag, D, and drag
coefficient, Cd, are derived at 390 and 400. These turbulent
boundary layer calculations use the one-seventh power law
Equations (4.36) and (4.37).

(4) Results are printed by lines 410 to 550.

(5) Two runs are shown. The first is with a laminar boundary layer
over the whole plate. The second is at a fairly high plate Reynolds
number with a transition Reynolds number at the 'typical' value of
5×10^5; the laminar layer covers less than 10% of the surface and
contributes less than 1% to the drag; at transition, the boundary
layer thickness increases by about 40%.

**Example 4.4   POHLHAUSEN: use of the Pohlhausen velocity
profile to calculate conditions in a laminar boundary layer with a
specified external velocity gradient**

Pohlhausen's Equation (4.21) uses the parameter

$$\lambda = \frac{\delta}{\nu} \frac{dU_1}{dx}$$

to describe the velocity profile in a laminar boundary layer outside
which there is a velocity (or pressure) gradient dU_1/dx. From this
profile, the following expressions for surface shear stress (4.1),
displacement thickness (4.2) and momentum thickness (4.3) may
be obtained in terms of λ:

$$\tau_w = \frac{\mu U_1}{\delta} \left(2 + \frac{\lambda}{6} \right) \tag{1}$$

$$\delta^* = \left(\frac{3}{10} - \frac{\lambda}{120} \right) \delta \tag{2}$$

$$\theta = \left(\frac{37}{315} - \frac{\lambda}{945} - \frac{\lambda^2}{9072} \right) \delta \tag{3}$$

Substitution into the momentum integral Equation (4.4) gives,
after some manipulation

$$\frac{d(\theta^2/\nu)}{dx} = \frac{F(\lambda)}{U_1} \tag{4}$$

where

$$F(\lambda) = 2\left(\frac{37}{315} - \frac{\lambda}{945} - \frac{\lambda^2}{9072}\right)\left(2 - \frac{116\lambda}{315} + \frac{79\lambda^2}{7560} + \frac{\lambda^3}{4536}\right)$$
(5)

Equation (4) provides a relation between momentum thickness θ and distance x from the boundary layer origin which will be integrated numerically by the computer program.

It can also be shown from Equation (3) and the definition of λ that

$$\frac{\theta^2}{\nu}\frac{dU_1}{dx} = \left(\frac{37}{315} - \frac{\lambda}{945} - \frac{\lambda^2}{9072}\right)^2\lambda$$
(6)

which provides an equation linking momentum thickness θ with λ. The details of the above analysis may be found in *Boundary Layer Theory* by Schlichting.

Equation (4) may be solved numerically if, (a) the external velocity U_1 and its derivative U_1' with respect to x are specified, and (b) initial conditions are known; Schlichting shows that, at an initial stagnation point

$$\lambda_0 = 7.052, \quad \left(\frac{\theta^2}{\nu}\right)_0 = \frac{0.077}{U_{1_0}'}$$

and

$$\left(\frac{d(\theta^2/\nu)}{dx}\right)_0 = \frac{-0.0652\ U_{1_0}''}{(U_{1_0}')^2}$$
(7)

where dashes denote derivatives with respect to distance x from the stagnation point.

The table below shows the distribution of external velocity and its derivative on part of the upper surface of an aerofoil over which the boundary layer is laminar for the first 50% of the chord.

x/c	0	0.05	0.10	0.15	0.20	0.25	0.30	0.35	0.40	0.45	0.50
U_1/U_0	0	0.9	1.0	1.03	1.05	1.065	1.075	1.085	1.095	1.105	1.115
$\dfrac{d(U_1/U_0)}{d(x/c)}$	25	9	1	0.5	0.35	0.25	0.2	0.2	0.2	0.2	0.2

where U_0 is freestream speed and c is aerofoil chord. The initial value of U_1' is zero at the forward stagnation point.

The following computer program finds boundary layer thicknesses, surface shear stresses and other parameters, from the aerofoil leading edge to the 50% chord point and also calculates skin friction drag.

```
10    Mu=.00001789
20    Ro=1.225
30    Nu=Mu/Ro
40    PRINT "PLEASE INPUT THE FREESTREAM SPEED AND THE AEROFOIL CHORD"
50    INPUT U0,C
60    PRINT U0,C
70    PRINT
80    Dx=.05*C
90    S=0
100   PRINT "   X      U     DU/DX   B L TH    DISP TH    MOM TH     H    SHEAR STR  LA
MDA"
110   PRINT " (M)   (M/S)  (M/SM)    (M)        (M)        (M)            (N/M^2)"
120   PRINT
130     DATA 0.25,.9,9,1,1,1.03,.5,1.05,.35,1.065,.25
140     DATA 1.075,.2,1.085,.2,1.095,.2,1.105,.2,1.115,.2
150   IMAGE D.DD,3X,DDD,3X,DDDD,3X,3(.DDDDDD,3X),D.DD,3X,DD.DD,3X,DD.DD
160   FOR I=0 TO 10
170     X=I*C/20
180     READ U,Ud
190     U=U*U0
200     Ud=Ud*U0/C
210     IF I<>0 THEN 270
220       La=7.052
230       Th=SQR(Nu*.077/Ud)
240       L=37/315-La/945-La*La/9072
250       Udd=0
260       GOTO 340
270     Th=SQR(Th*Th+Fu*Nu*Dx)
280       L=37/315-La/945-La*La/9072
290       N=L*L*La-Th*Th*Ud/Nu
300       N1=2*L*(-1/945-La/4536)*La+L*L
310       La=La-N/N1
320       IF ABS(N/N1)<.001 THEN 340
330       GOTO 280
340     Del=Th/L
350     Delst=(3/10-La/120)*Del
360     T0=Mu*U/Del*(2+La/6)
370     S=S+T0
380     H=Delst/Th
390     IF I<>0 THEN 420
400       Fu=-.0652*Udd/(Ud*Ud)
410       GOTO 440
420     F=2*L*(2-116*La/315+79/7560*La*La+2/9072*La*La*La)
430     Fu=F/U
440     PRINT USING 150;X;U;Ud;Del;Delst;Th;H;T0;La
450   NEXT I
460   PRINT
470   IMAGE 42A.DDD.DDDDD
480   PRINT USING 470;"FREESTREAM SPEED = ";U0
490   PRINT USING 470;"AEROFOIL CHORD = ";C
500   PRINT USING 470;"FRICTION DRAG = ";S*Dx
510   PRINT USING 470;"FRICTION DRAG COEFFICIENT BASED ON 50%C = ";S*.05/(.5*Ro*
U0*U0*.5)
520   END
```

```
RUN
PLEASE INPUT THE FREESTREAM SPEED AND THE AEROFOIL CHORD
   60        .4
```

X (M)	U (M/S)	DU/DX (M/SM)	B L TH (M)	DISP TH (M)	MOM TH (M)	H	SHEAR STR (N/M^2)	LAMDA
0.00	0	3750	.000166	.000040	.000017	2.31	0.00	7.05
.02	54	1350	.000151	.000043	.000017	2.46	15.05	2.11
.04	60	150	.000375	.000108	.000043	2.49	6.42	1.44
.06	62	75	.000515	.000149	.000060	2.49	4.78	1.36
.08	63	53	.000624	.000180	.000072	2.49	4.03	1.40
.10	64	38	.000714	.000206	.000083	2.49	3.55	1.31
.12	65	30	.000794	.000230	.000092	2.50	3.22	1.29
.14	65	30	.000869	.000249	.000100	2.48	3.03	1.55
.16	66	30	.000935	.000266	.000108	2.47	2.89	1.79
.18	66	30	.000993	.000281	.000114	2.46	2.79	2.02
.20	67	30	.001045	.000294	.000120	2.46	2.72	2.24

```
FREESTREAM SPEED =                        60.00000
AEROFOIL CHORD =                            .40000
FRICTION DRAG =                             .96966
FRICTION DRAG COEFFICIENT BASED ON 50%C =   .00220
```

Program notes

(1) The aerofoil is assumed to be operating in standard sea level conditions in lines 10 to 30, and the operator inputs speed and chord length at 40 to 60. Line 90 sets the initial value of the variable S, which will be used to accumulate (at line 370) shear stresses along the surface, to zero. The given non-dimensional values of velocity and velocity gradient over the surface are stored in the DATA statements of lines 130 and 140.

(2) The calculations at the eleven aerofoil stations from leading stagnation point to 50% chord are contained in the FOR-NEXT loop from 160 to 450. The non-dimensional velocities and gradients are READ at 180 and converted to dimensional values at 190 and 200. At the forward stagnation point (I = 0), initial values as specified by Equations (7) are stated from 220 to 260. At downstream points, Equation (4) is used at line 270 to calculate momentum thickness θ; this is followed at lines 280 to 330 by a Newton–Raphson solution of Equation (6) to get the value of λ (the starting value of λ in this iteration is taken to be that of the previous aerofoil station). Lines 340 to 380 calculate boundary layer thickness, displacement thickness, surface shear stress, accumulated shear stress and shape factor using Equations (1) to (3). Finally, F/U1 (represented by the variable Fu) is found, using an initial value from Equations (7) at the stagnation point in line 400, and using Equation (5) at downstream points in lines 420 and 430.

(3) Results are printed from 440 to 510 employing PRINT USING statements to control layout and decimal point position. The IMAGEs called by these statements are at 150 and 470.

(4) One RUN is shown. Boundary layer thicknesses increase monotonically from the leading edge (apart from the initial fall in δ which is not physically significant). Shear stress has a maximum just downstream of the leading edge and λ shows a generally downward trend. The pressure gradient is favourable throughout and the boundary layer shape factor H does not change much.

(5) Only the leading half chord of the aerofoil has been considered in this example because the mid-chord point represents the practical limit to the distance over which a favourable pressure gradient may be maintained on a real subsonic aerofoil surface. Downstream of this point, an adverse pressure gradient will inevitably trigger transition and a quite different program of calculations would be needed for the turbulent boundary layer.

However, the student will find it instructive to insert additional DATA values representing typical values of velocity and velocity gradient over the rear of the aerofoil (the same speeds with gradients of opposite sign to those on the forward section of the aerofoil would suffice) and to make the necessary small adjustments to the program. A RUN would then show λ decreasing to negative values, eventually reaching −12 and identifying the laminar separation point.

(6) Pohlhausen calculations are generally found to give good agreement with measurements up to the minimum pressure point, but laminar separation point predictions are unreliable.

PROBLEMS

(4.1) Write a program which will input freestream conditions and the boundary layer thickness at a particular point on the surface of a flat plate and which will then tabulate the velocity and total pressure distribution across the boundary layer at intervals of 0.05 thickness. The operator is to be given the option of seeing the velocity profiles of: (a) a laminar boundary layer calculated from the Pohlhausen equation, (b) a turbulent boundary layer calculated from the one seventh power law, or (c) both laminar and turbulent profiles side by side. If your computer has a graphics facility, extend the program to display graphs of these profiles.

(4.2) The working section of a wind tunnel is frequently designed to diverge slightly in order to avoid a streamwise pressure gradient due to boundary layer growth on the working section walls. Write a program which will input: (a) the entry height and width, and length of a rectangular working section, (b) the assumed boundary layer thickness at entry to the working section, and (c) the tunnel normal working speed, and then output the width and height required at the working section exit to produce zero streamwise pressure gradient in an empty tunnel. The boundary layer is to be assumed turbulent throughout with a one-seventh power law velocity profile; the program is to allow entry boundary layer thickness to be specified as either 99% thickness, displacement thickness or momentum thickness.

(4.3) A convenient formula (due to Prandtl) for evaluating the drag on a flat plate with part laminar and part turbulent boundary layer is

$$C_f = \frac{0.074}{Re_L^{1/5}} - \frac{A}{Re_L}$$

where $10^5 < \mathrm{Re}_L < 5 \times 10^6$ and A depends on the transition Reynolds number as follows:

Re_{tr}	3×10^5	5×10^5	10^6	3×10^6
A	1050	1700	3300	8700

Write a program which contains these values as DATA and which will input plate area and transition Reynolds number to give friction drag and friction drag coefficient.

(4.4) Write a program which will input dimensions and freestream conditions and then calculate the laminar skin friction drag on a triangular flat plate by summing the drag of strips of appropriate width parallel to the freestream. The plate triangle is isosceles with vertex pointing directly upstream.

(4.5) Extend the program in Problem (4.4) to allow for transition on each strip at some specified transition Reynolds number. Strips will then be either completely laminar if near the triangle tips or laminar/turbulent if near the centre line.

(4.6) An approximate method, due to Thwaites, for finding laminar boundary layer properties with an external pressure gradient expresses momentum thickness θ at distance x from the leading edge of a surface as

$$\theta^2 = \frac{0.45\nu}{(U_1^6)_x} \int_0^x U_1^5 \, dx$$

and the method also shows that laminar separation occurs when

$$\frac{dU_1}{dx} \frac{\theta^2}{\nu} = -0.082$$

$U_1(x)$ is the local freestream velocity.

Write a program which will evaluate the integral numerically for a range of values of x, and hence find the separation point on an aerofoil section over which the local freestream velocity can be approximated by

$$U_1 = 1.25 \, U_0 \sin \frac{\pi x}{c}$$

with U_0 = freestream velocity = 100 m/s and c = chord = 1.2 m. Note that if $U_1 \simeq \beta x$ when x is small, as near the stagnation point, then from the integral above it may readily be shown that

$$\theta^2_{x=0} = \frac{0.45\nu}{6\beta}$$

i.e. θ is not zero at the origin.

Chapter 5

Aerofoil section theory

ESSENTIAL THEORY

5.1 Introduction

An aerofoil section (henceforward abbreviated to aerofoil) is a closed plane curve of a shape capable of generating a useful lift force with minimum drag when placed in a uniform stream; it is the shape found when a wing is cut by a plane perpendicular to its spanwise axis.

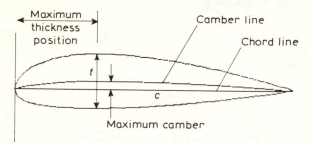

Figure 5.1 Aerofoil geometry

A major requirement of the aerofoil shape is the avoidance of flow separation which produces high pressure drag, and consequently the aerofoil will normally operate over a limited positive and negative incidence range.

5.1.1 Reynolds number and Mach number

The streamline pattern around a body in an inviscid, incompressible fluid depends solely on the body shape and attitude to the flow (incidence). In a viscous fluid, the pattern depends also on Reynolds number, Re $= \rho U c / \mu$. The representative length, c, is usually taken, in aerofoil theory, to be the chord. In a compressible fluid, the streamline pattern around a body also depends on the Mach number M $= U/a$.

5.2   Aerofoil properties

Forces

The total force per unit span, R, acting on a body in a moving fluid may be resolved into two perpendicular components:

(1) LIFT (L)   – the component perpendicular to the relative flow
(2) DRAG (D)   – the component parallel to the relative flow

These forces act at the *centre of pressure* (CP), the position of which is dependent on the body shape, incidence, Reynolds number and Mach number. The lift and drag coefficients C_L and C_D are defined

$$C_L = L/\tfrac{1}{2}\rho U^2 S \quad \text{and} \quad C_D = D/\tfrac{1}{2}\rho U^2 s \qquad (5.1)$$

where S is a representative area. These coefficients are non-dimensional and consequently are only dependent on other non-dimensional factors, such as body shape, incidence, Reynolds number, Mach number (and any other dimensionless parameters which may be relevant to the flow). For bluff bodies, i.e. bodies which cause a large disturbance and have a large wake, S is usually taken as the cross sectional area perpendicular to the flow; for aerodynamically well shaped or 'streamlined' bodies, it is the plan area parallel to the flow.

Moments

The resultant force R acting on a body will exert a moment per unit span, M, about a general point X. The moment coefficient acting about X is

$$C_{M_x} = M/\tfrac{1}{2}\rho U^2 S\ell \qquad (5.2)$$

where ℓ is a representative length – usually the chord for an aerofoil. C_{M_x} is dimensionless and is dependent on the non-dimensional parameters which determine lift coefficient, as well as the position of the origin of moments.

Lift

In order to produce a lift force L when in a uniform stream U, circulation Γ must be present around the aerofoil. In a real fluid, this bound vortex changes its strength whenever the freestream speed or aerofoil incidence change, as a reaction to the creation and shedding of 'starting vortices' at the sharp trailing edge.

Vorticity is shed until the Kutta condition is satisfied, i.e. there is smooth flow in a streamwise direction off both upper and lower aerofoil surfaces, and in a perfect fluid, the trailing edge is then a stagnation point. A simple analysis of a particular type of aerofoil, the Joukowsi aerofoil (see Section 5.3), shows, that for a symmetrical aerofoil, the Kutta condition is satisfied when

$$\Gamma = \pi c U \alpha \qquad (5.3)$$

where α is the incidence. Combining $L = \rho U \Gamma$ with Equations (5.1) and (5.3) gives

$$C_L = 2\pi \alpha \qquad (5.4)$$

for a symmetrical aerofoil, i.e. there is a linear relationship (which also holds for a cambered aerofoil) between C_L and α up to the incidence at which a flow separation occurs on the upper surface; this happens at about 15° incidence and the aerofoil is then said to be *stalled*. The value of C_L at stall, the aerofoil $C_{L_{max}}$, is a most important parameter in aircraft operation: it is Reynolds number and Mach number dependent. The lift curve slope 2π is not achieved in practice and a commonly assumed value at low Mach number is 5.7 per radian or 0.1 per degree.

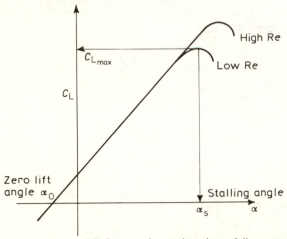

Figure 5.2 $C_L \sim \alpha$ of a cambered aerofoil

Centre of pressure

The centre of pressure position of a symmetrical aerofoil in inviscid, incompressible flow is at the quarter chord point; boundary layer effects may result in a small forward movement by

1 or 2% of c. The CP of a cambered aerofoil is at a large distance downstream at zero lift, and it moves forward as incidence increases, towards the quarter chord point.

Drag

The drag force D is the sum of skin friction and pressure drag. At low Mach number and low incidences, the friction drag is a large proportion of total drag. At stall, the separation from the upper surface leads to a large wake and large pressure drag (much greater than friction drag). At high Mach number when shock waves are present, an additional pressure drag, called wave drag, acts on the aerofoil.

Pitching moments

At the zero lift incidence α_0, the pressure distribution produces a pure couple M_0 which is a function of camber; positive camber gives negative (nose down) moment and the zero lift pitching moment coefficient is:

$$C_{M_0} = M_0 / \tfrac{1}{2}\rho U^2 S c \qquad (5.5)$$

Pitching moments about a general point vary linearly with incidence (and C_L) up to stall.

Aerodynamic centre

There is a point in the aerofoil where pitching moment is the same at all angles of incidence and equal to M_0; this is the *aerodynamic centre* of the aerofoil and, at low M, it lies within 1 or 2% of the quarter chord point. The moment of the lift force (at the centre of pressure) about a general point X is equal to the sum of M_0 and the moment, about X, of the lift as if it acted at the aerodynamic centre.

5.3 Joukowski aerofoils

5.3.1 Joukowski transformation

A point represented by the complex number, $z = x + jy$, in the z plane may be transformed into a point in the Z plane by means of a transformation: $Z = f(z)$. Sets of points forming curves in the z plane will transform into different curves in the Z plane. The transformation:

$$Z = z + c^2/z \qquad (5.6)$$

where c is a positive real number, is called the *Joukowski* transformation and is a particular example of a general class of transformations called conformal transformations which have the following properties:

(1) If ψ = constant and ϕ = constant represent sets of streamlines and corresponding equipotentials of a flow in the z plane, then their transformations in the Z plane will also be streamlines and corresponding equipotentials of some different flow.

(2) Stagnation points in the z plane transform into stagnation points in the Z plane.

(3) As $z \rightarrow \infty$, then $Z \rightarrow \infty$, i.e. a uniform stream at a large distance from the origin in the z plane transforms into a uniform stream of the same magnitude and direction in the Z plane.

(4) The circulation around any closed circuit in the z plane is the same as the circulation around the corresponding circuit in the Z plane.

Separating the real and imaginary parts of the Joukowski Equation (5.6) gives the Cartesian form:

$$X = x[1 + c^2/(x^2 + y^2)]$$
$$Y = y[1 + c^2/(x^2 + y^2)] \tag{5.7}$$

and the fluid speed Q in the Z plane is related to the speed q in the z plane:

$$Q = \frac{q}{\left| \dfrac{dZ}{dz} \right|} = \frac{q}{|1 - c^2/z^2|} \tag{5.8}$$

5.3.2   Joukowski aerofoils

A circle of radius a is transformed into an aerofoil shape by the Joukowski transformation provided that the transformation singular point at $z = +c$ lies on the circle, and the other singular point at $z = -c$ is either within or on the circle. This aerofoil which has a sharp (cusped) trailing edge is called a Joukowski aerofoil; its shape depends on the position of the centre of the circle in the z plane as follows:

Circle centre position in z plane	Aerofoil shape in Z plane (chord = 4a)
Origin	Flat plate
On $0y$ axis	Cambered plate
On $0x$ axis	Symmetrical aerofoil
Offset from both axes	Cambered aerofoil

The streamlines of the flow of a uniform stream around a circle at incidence α in the z plane, are transformed, in the Z plane, into streamlines around an aerofoil at incidence α. Addition of circulation to the flow round the cylinder introduces circulation of the same strength round the aerofoil. The positions of the stagnation points on the aerofoil are determined by the aerofoil camber, the incidence α and the circulation Γ. The lift is $\rho U\Gamma$.

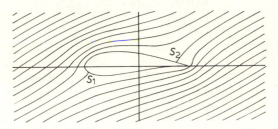

Figure 5.3 Aerofoil in Z plane at 30° incidence with zero circulation

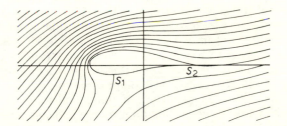

Figure 5.4 Aerofoil in Z plane at 30° incidence with sufficient circulation to satisfy the Kutta condition

Now, in a real fluid at high Reynolds number, flow around the sharp trailing edge towards the upper surface stagnation point S_2 in Figure 5.3 is not possible, and, after a change in incidence or speed, flow separates at the trailing edge generating 'starting vortices' which are shed downstream. Simultaneously, equal and opposite bound circulation is created around the aerofoil causing S_2 to move towards the trailing edge. When S_2 arrives at the trailing edge, the fluid leaves both upper and lower surfaces smoothly in a streamwise direction and vortex shedding ceases; bound circulation exists around the aerofoil and the flow is said to satisfy the Kutta condition, as shown in Figure 5.4.

To make the trailing edge a stagnation point, requires circulation around the aerofoil of magnitude

$$\Gamma = 4\pi a U(\alpha + \beta) \tag{5.9}$$

where $-\beta$ (the zero lift incidence) is a function of aerofoil camber. Then

$$C_L = \rho U \Gamma / \tfrac{1}{2} \rho U^2 c = 2\pi(\alpha + \beta) \tag{5.10}$$

with $c \simeq 4a$. See Figure 5.2 where $\alpha_0 = -\beta$.

Speeds in the aerofoil flow may be calculated from Equation (5.8) using speeds at corresponding points in the flow around a cylinder (see Equations (3.16) to (3.19)); pressures are then available from Bernoulli's equation.

5.4   Source and doublet distributions

Using the methods of Chapter 3, it can be shown that the combination of a uniform stream with either a source and equal sink, or with a doublet, produces the external flow around a closed body (Rankine oval or cylinder). More generally, if a number of isolated sources and sinks of equal total strength (and/or doublets) are appropriately distributed along the $0x$ axis in a uniform stream, a variety of closed symmetrical shapes may be created and this idea may be extended to include continuously variable distributions of elements. Provided the total source and sink strengths are equal, the flow around any symmetrical contour may be constructed by distributing elements along the $0x$ axis, and the flow around a cambered body may be obtained by a distribution along a curved 'camber' line. To determine the distribution needed to produce a prescribed body shape requires solution of an integral equation which is generally performed numerically to the required degree of accuracy.

5.4.1   Linear doublet distribution

A continuous doublet distribution along $0x$ of density $\mu(x)$ between $x = a$ and $x = b$ may be approximated by N discrete doublet elements of strengths $\mu_1, \mu_2, \ldots, \mu_N$ equally spaced between a and b at points $(x_1, 0), (x_2, 0), \ldots, (x_N, 0)$.

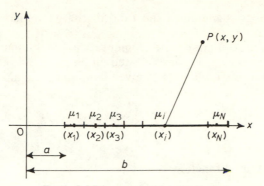

Figure 5.5 Discrete doublet distribution

With a uniform stream superimposed, the stream function ψ at a general point P (x, y) is

$$\psi = Uy - \sum_{i=1}^{N} \frac{\mu_i y}{2\pi \left[(x - x_i)^2 + (y - y_i)^2\right]} \qquad (5.11)$$

Now, on the prescribed body surface, $\psi = 0$, and if this condition is applied to Equation (5.11) at N points, called control points, known to lie on the body surface, then the resulting N simultaneous equations may be solved for the N unknown μ_i. The selection of control points requires some care for best results; to increase accuracy (and computational demands) N may be increased.

5.5 Source panel methods

A source panel in two dimensions is a finite segment of a straight line L over which there is a continuous, constant source (or sink) distribution. The source strength per unit length is called the

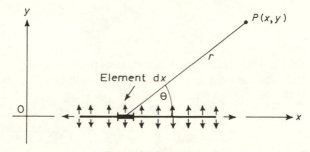

Figure 5.6 Source panel

source density, denoted λ; the fluid discharge velocity from the panel is $\lambda/2$.

The source strength on the element dx is λdx so that, using the stream function of a source stated in Section 3.4, the stream function at a general point P is given by the integral along the line L:

$$\psi = \int_L \frac{\lambda \theta dx}{2\pi}$$
(5.12)

and the potential function

$$\phi = \int_L \frac{\lambda \ln r \, dx}{2\pi}$$
(5.13)

5.5.1 Body panels in two dimensions

The curved surface of a prescribed two-dimensional aerofoil or body in a uniform stream U may be approximated by a finite number, N, of source panels, each of which is given a source distribution of density λ_i.

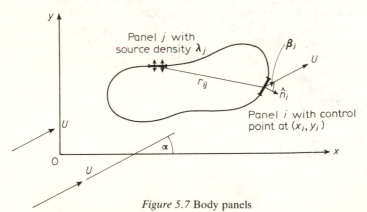

Figure 5.7 Body panels

If the mid-point of each panel is a control point with coordinates (x_i, y_i), then the velocity potential at control point i due to all N source panels is

$$\phi = \sum_{j=1}^{N} \int_{Panel\ j} \frac{\lambda_j \ln r_{ij} \, ds_j}{2\pi}$$
(5.14)

where the N integrations run over the lengths of each panel, and

$$r_{ij} = [(x_i - x_j)^2 + (y_i - y_j)^2]^{1/2} \qquad (5.15)$$

If the body is now placed at incidence α in a freestream U, then the velocity potential at control point i is

$$\phi = Ux \cos \alpha + Uy \sin \alpha + \frac{1}{2\pi} \sum_{j=1}^{N} \int_j \lambda_j \ln r_{ij} \, \mathrm{d}s_j \qquad (5.16)$$

On the body surface, and therefore at each control point, the fluid velocity perpendicular to the panel is zero:

$$\frac{\partial \phi}{\partial n_i} = 0 \qquad (5.17)$$

where n_i is in the direction perpendicular to panel i.

Differentiating Equation (5.16), and using the result that fluid discharge velocity at control point i due to source panel i is $\lambda_i/2$, gives N equations:

$$2\pi U \cos \beta_i + \pi\lambda_i + \sum_{\substack{j=1 \\ i \neq j}}^{N} \lambda_j \int \frac{\partial}{\partial n_i} (\ln r_{ij}) \, \mathrm{d}s_j = 0 \qquad (5.18)$$

where β_i is the angle between the freestream and the normal to panel i (see Figure 5.7). Solution of the N simultaneous equations for values of λ_i will ultimately give the flow velocities, pressures and body forces.

5.5.2   Body panels in three dimensions

A three-dimensional body surface may be represented by a number of plane surface elements, not necessarily of regular shape, each carrying a control point which is usually at its centroid. Each plane element is given a source distribution of uniform density and unknown strength. The analysis then follows the same steps as in the two-dimensional case above; line integrals now become surface integrals.

5.6   Thin aerofoil theory

5.6.1   Aerofoil theory

Since thickness plays an insignificant part in the generation of lift, an aerofoil shape may be simplified by reducing its thickness to zero so that it is represented simply by its camber line. Circulation

$\gamma(x)$, needed to produce lift, is distributed continuously along the camber line producing a vortex sheet which has a local circulation density adjusted to ensure: (a) that the camber line is a streamline, and (b) that the Kutta condition is satisfied at the trailing edge.

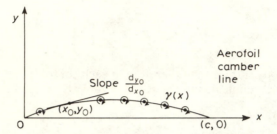

Figure 5.8 Aerofoil represented by a vortex distribution along the camber line

The two conditions on $\gamma(x)$ result in the equations

$$U\left[\alpha - \left(\frac{dy}{dx}\right)_0\right] = \frac{1}{2\pi} \int_0^c \frac{\gamma(x)\, dx}{x_0 - x} \qquad (5.19)$$

and

$$\gamma(c) = 0 \qquad (5.20)$$

These are the thin aerofoil equations. The velocity difference between upper and lower surfaces is $\gamma(x)$ and the pressure difference $\rho U \gamma(x)$. The lift force L is

$$L = \rho U \int_0^c \gamma(x)\, dx \qquad (5.21)$$

and the pitching moment M_{LE} about the leading edge is

$$M_{LE} = -\rho U \int_0^c x\gamma(x)\, dx \qquad (5.22)$$

5.6.2   Solution of the thin aerofoil equations

An important coordinate transformation for solving Equations (5.19) and (5.20) is

$$x = \frac{c}{2}(1 - \cos\theta) \qquad (5.23)$$

and the equations then become

$$U\left[\alpha - \left(\frac{dy}{dx}\right)_0\right] = \frac{1}{2\pi}\int_0^\pi \frac{\gamma(\theta)\sin\theta\,d\theta}{\cos\theta - \cos\theta_0} \quad (5.24)$$

and

$$\gamma(\pi) = 0 \quad (5.25)$$

The general function $\gamma(\theta)$ which satisfies Equations (5.24) and (5.25) may be written:

$$\gamma(\theta) = 2UA_0\frac{(1 + \cos\theta)}{\sin\theta} + 2U\sum_{n=1}^{\infty}A_n\sin n\theta \quad (5.26)$$

A_0 contains both incidence and camber terms

$$A_0 = \alpha - \frac{1}{\pi}\int_0^\pi \frac{dy}{dx}\,d\theta \quad (5.27)$$

$$= \alpha - A_0' \quad (5.28)$$

where

$$A_0' = \frac{1}{\pi}\int_0^\pi \frac{dy}{dx}\,d\theta \quad (5.29)$$

is the camber term, and the A_n coefficients are functions of camber only, given by

$$A_n = \frac{2}{\pi}\int_0^\pi \frac{dy}{dx}\cos n\theta\,d\theta \quad (5.30)$$

Now, from Equations (5.21), (5.26), (5.28) and (5.30), lift L is given by

$$C_L = 2\pi\alpha - \pi(2A_0' - A_1) \quad (5.31)$$

Thin aerofoil theory thus predicts a lift curve slope of 2π/rad and a zero lift incidence of $\alpha_0 = (2A_0' - A_1)/2$.

The pitching moment coefficient about the quarter chord point (aerodynamic centre) is

$$C_{M_{1/4}} = \frac{\pi}{4}(A_2 - A_1) = C_{M_0} \qquad (5.32)$$

This is a function of camber and is independent of incidence. The centre of pressure position relative to the leading edge is

$$x_{CP} = \frac{c}{4}\left[\frac{2A_0 + 2A_1 - A_2}{2A_0 + A_1}\right] \qquad (5.33)$$

Symmetrical aerofoil

For a symmetrical aerofoil, which reduces, in thin aerofoil theory, to a flat plate, $A_0 = \alpha$ and $A_n = 0$ for all other n, so that

$$\gamma(\theta) = 2U\alpha(1 + \cos\theta)/\sin\theta \qquad (5.34)$$

Trailing edge flap

Providing angles remain small, the effect of trailing edge flap deflection through angle η may be obtained by adding to the above basic results, contributions to C_L and C_M from the aerofoil shown in Figure 5.9.

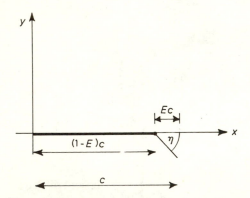

Figure 5.9 The aerofoil representing flap deflection

At the hinge point, $\theta = \phi$ where

$$(1 - \cos\phi)/2 = 1 - E$$

Values of the A_n coefficients for this flap are

$$A_0 = \frac{\eta}{\pi}(\pi - \phi) \qquad (5.35)$$

$$A_n = \frac{2\eta \sin n\phi}{n\pi} \quad \text{for } n \geq 1 \tag{5.36}$$

The flap's contribution to C_L is therefore

$$\Delta C_L = 2\eta (\pi - \phi + \sin \phi) \tag{5.37}$$

and to C_M is

$$\Delta C_{M_{1/4}} = \frac{\eta}{4} (\sin 2\phi - 2 \sin \phi) \tag{5.38}$$

and to the zero lift incidence angle is

$$\Delta \alpha_0 = -\frac{\eta}{\pi} (\pi - \phi + \sin \phi) \tag{5.39}$$

All these additional flap terms are directly proportional to η, the flap deflection angle.

5.7 Boundary layer effects

The effects of boundary layer thickness an aerofoil performance may be accounted for by adding the boundary layer displacement thickness to the basic aerofoil profile. Calculations on boundary layer thickness require prior information on surface pressure gradients which are themselves unknown until displacement thickness is determined. This circular problem is solved iteratively, starting with the calculation of the surface pressure distribution on the specified aerofoil with no boundary layer. With this surface pressure information available, the displacement thickness may now be found and added to the basic aerofoil thickness; the resulting modified aerofoil now becomes the starting point for a new round of calculations of pressure distribution and displacement thickness, and the iteration is continued until the solution converges to the accuracy required.

5.8 Subsonic compressibility effects

The two-dimensional equation describing compressible, irrotational flow around an aerofoil is non-linear:

$$\left(1 - \frac{u^2}{a^2}\right) \frac{\partial u}{\partial x} + \left(1 - \frac{v^2}{a^2}\right) \frac{\partial v}{\partial y} - \frac{2uv}{a^2} \frac{\partial u}{\partial y} = 0 \tag{5.40}$$

General analytical solutions are not possible and the principle of superposition used in linear theories to build up complicated flows from the sum of two or more simple flows, cannot be applied.

Using a perturbation velocity potential ϕ, this equation may be simplified for a slender aerofoil moving at speed U and Mach number M along the $0x$ axis to

$$(1 - M^2) \frac{\partial^2 \phi}{\partial x^2} + \frac{\partial^2 \phi}{\partial y^2} = 0 \qquad (5.41)$$

which may be transformed, using the Affine transformation

$$x' = x/\beta \quad ; \quad y' = y \qquad (5.42)$$

where $\beta = (1 - M^2)^{1/2}$, to Laplace's equation

$$\nabla^2 \phi = 0 \qquad (5.43)$$

This equation is satisfied by the incompressible velocity potential function (see Equation 3.14). If an incompressible solution to Equation (3.14) for a specified aerofoil is known, then the corresponding compressible solution to Equation (5.41) can easily be found by applying the reverse Affine transformation, Equation (5.42).

The pressure coefficient C_p in compressible flow can be obtained from the corresponding pressure coefficient C_{p_0} in incompressible flow:

$$C_p = C_{p_0}/\beta \qquad (5.44)$$

provided the slender condition is satisfied, i.e. perturbations are small; this condition is not satisfied near a stagnation point or when strong shock waves are present. The term $\beta = (1 - M^2)^{1/2}$ is known as the Prandtl–Glauert factor.

Integration of the surface pressures given by Equation (5.44) over an aerofoil surface results in

$$C_L = C_{L_0}/\beta \qquad (5.45)$$

$$C_D = C_{D_0}/\beta \qquad (5.46)$$

$$C_M = C_{M_0}/\beta \qquad (5.47)$$

where the suffix o refers to incompressible conditions and Equation (5.46) applies to pressure, and not friction, drag.

5.8.1 Shock waves

When shock waves are present in a transonic flow, solutions to Equation (5.40) must be found using numerical methods. As the position of the shocks is very sensitive to small changes in aerofoil effective contour, the numerical technique selected must be capable of producing accurate solutions and ample computer capability is normally essential in this difficult flow regime.

WORKED EXAMPLES

Example 5.1   TUNRESULT: the reduction of wind tunnel lift, pitching moment and incidence results

Measurements, made in a wind tunnel, of the variation of lift and pitching moment with incidence, require correction for tunnel interference effects and reduction to non-dimensional coefficient form. This program inputs results of tests carried out on the two-dimensional flow over an aerofoil which spans the tunnel from wall to wall. The test measurements are:

Incidence (degrees)	Lift/span (N/m)	Moment/span (Nm/m)
−4	−22.77	−0.415
−2	−8.14	−0.378
0	6.37	−0.339
2	21.01	−0.300
4	34.22	−0.262
6	49.33	−0.207
8	63.78	−0.183
10	78.03	−0.134
12	91.44	−0.095

Tunnel speed = 30 m/s. Aerofoil chord = 0.17 m. Moments were measured about the aerofoil quarter chord point. Sea level conditions

The corrections for wind tunnel interference effects on a two-dimensional flow in a closed wind tunnel are given by

$$\Delta C_L = - \frac{\pi^2}{48} \left(\frac{c}{h} \right)^2 C_{L_T}$$

$$\Delta C_M = \frac{\pi^2}{192} \left(\frac{c}{h} \right)^2 C_{L_T}$$

$$\Delta \alpha = \frac{\pi}{96} \left(\frac{c}{h} \right)^2 (C_{L_T} + 4 C_{M_T})$$

where suffix T denotes measured tunnel values, c is aerofoil chord and h is tunnel height, equal to 0.95 m.

The program inputs the measured values, and calculates and tabulates corrected results. Using least squares, the best straight line is fitted to the $C_L \sim \alpha$ values and to the $C_M \sim C_L$ values and the slopes and intercepts are printed. Finally, the position of the aerodynamic centre is found using

$$h_0 - d = - \frac{dC_M}{dC_L}$$

where h_0 and d are, respectively, non-dimensional distances from the aerofoil leading edge of the aerodynamic centre and the origin of pitching moments; finally, the program tabulates the variation of centre of pressure position with incidence.

The program complements Example 2.4 which deals with balance corrections.

```
10    DIM A(25),Cm(25),Cl(25)
20    Ro=1.225
30    PRINT "PLEASE INPUT SPEED,CHORD AND TUNNEL HEIGHT ";
40    INPUT U,C,Ht
50    PRINT U,C,Ht
60    PRINT "PLEASE INPUT THE POINT ABOUT WHICH PITCHING MOMENTS WERE"
70    PRINT "  MEASURED AS A FRACTION OF THE CHORD ";
80    INPUT D
90    PRINT D
100   PRINT "HOW MANY INCIDENCE POINTS WERE THERE? ";
110   INPUT N
120   PRINT N
130   PRINT
140   L0=1/2*Ro*U*U*C
150   M0=L0*C
160   Sa=0
170   Sl=0
180   Sm=0
190   Sal=0
200   Slm=0
210   Saa=0
220   Sll=0
230   IMAGE DD.DDD,12X
240   FOR I=1 TO N
250     PRINT "INPUT MEASURED INCIDENCE (DEG), LIFT AND P MOMENT    ";
260     INPUT A1,L1,M1
270     PRINT A1,L1,M1
280     Cl1=L1/L0
290     Cm1=M1/M0
300     A(I)=A1+PI/96*(C/Ht)^2*(Cl1+4*Cm1)*180/PI
310     Cm(I)=Cm1+PI*PI/192*(C/Ht)^2*Cl1
320     Cl(I)=Cl1-PI*PI/48*(C/Ht)^2*Cl1
330     Sa=Sa+A(I)
340     Sl=Sl+Cl(I)
350     Sm=Sm+Cm(I)
360     Sal=Sal+A(I)*Cl(I)
370     Slm=Slm+Cl(I)*Cm(I)
380     Saa=Saa+A(I)*A(I)
390     Sll=Sll+Cl(I)*Cl(I)
400   NEXT I
410   PRINT
420   PRINT "CORRECTED RESULTS"
430   PRINT "-----------------"
440   PRINT "INCIDENCE       LIFT COEFFT      MOMENT COEFFT    C OF P POSN(FRAC O
F C)"
450   FOR I=1 TO N
460     PRINT USING 230;A(I),Cl(I),Cm(I),(D-Cm(I)/Cl(I))
470   NEXT I
480   PRINT
490   Lcs=(N*Sal-Sa*Sl)/(N*Saa-Sa*Sa)
500   A0=-(Sl*Saa-Sa*Sal)/(N*Saa-Sa*Sa)/Lcs
510   Ms=(N*Slm-Sl*Sm)/(N*Sll-Sl*Sl)
520   Cm0=(Sm*Sll-Sl*Slm)/(N*Sll-Sl*Sl)
530   PRINT USING "19A,D.DDD,11A";"LIFT CURVE SLOPE = ";Lcs;" PER DEGREE"
540   PRINT USING "18A,DD.DDD,4A";"ZERO LIFT ANGLE = ";A0;" DEG"
550   PRINT USING "10A,D.DDD";"DCM/DCL = ";Ms
560   PRINT USING "35A,D.DDDD";"ZERO LIFT PITCHING MOMENT COEFFT = ";Cm0
570   PRINT USING "25A,D.DDD,26A";"AERODYNAMIC CENTRE IS AT ";(D-Ms);" CHORD AFT
OF LEADING EDGE"
580   END
```

```
RUN
PLEASE INPUT SPEED,CHORD AND TUNNEL HEIGHT   30      .17       .95
PLEASE INPUT THE POINT ABOUT WHICH PITCHING MOMENTS WERE
   MEASURED AS A FRACTION OF THE CHORD   .25
HOW MANY INCIDENCE POINTS WERE THERE?  9

INPUT MEASURED INCIDENCE (DEG), LIFT AND P MOMENT   -4     -22.77     -.415
INPUT MEASURED INCIDENCE (DEG), LIFT AND P MOMENT   -2      -8.14     -.378
INPUT MEASURED INCIDENCE (DEG), LIFT AND P MOMENT    0       6.37     -.339
INPUT MEASURED INCIDENCE (DEG), LIFT AND P MOMENT    2      21.01     -.3
INPUT MEASURED INCIDENCE (DEG), LIFT AND P MOMENT    4      34.22     -.262
INPUT MEASURED INCIDENCE (DEG), LIFT AND P MOMENT    6      49.22     -.207
INPUT MEASURED INCIDENCE (DEG), LIFT AND P MOMENT    8      63.78     -.183
INPUT MEASURED INCIDENCE (DEG), LIFT AND P MOMENT   10      78.03     -.134
INPUT MEASURED INCIDENCE (DEG), LIFT AND P MOMENT   12      91.44     -.095

CORRECTED RESULTS
-----------------
INCIDENCE        LIFT COEFFT      MOMENT COEFFT     C OF P POSN(FRAC OF C)
-4.021              -.241             -.026               .140
-2.011              -.086             -.024              -.027
 -.001               .068             -.021               .563
 2.009               .223             -.018               .333
 4.018               .363             -.016               .294
 6.028               .522             -.012               .273
 8.038               .676             -.010               .265
10.048               .827             -.007               .259
12.057               .969             -.004               .254

LIFT CURVE SLOPE =  .075 PER DEGREE
ZERO LIFT ANGLE =  -.870 DEG
DCM/DCL =  .018
ZERO LIFT PITCHING MOMENT COEFFT = -.0223
AERODYNAMIC CENTRE IS AT  .232 CHORD AFT OF LEADING EDGE
```

Program notes

(1) The arrays declared in line 10 will be used at lines 300, 310 and 320 to store corrected values of incidence, C_L and C_M. Lines 20 to 120 take in general information on the tests. Lines 140 and 150 calculate the non-dimensionalizing factors for lift and moment. Lines 160 to 220 set to zero the variables S used to accumulate the statistical sums required for calculating regression lines of C_L on α and C_M on C_L. Sa accumulates incidence; Sll accumulates C_L squared; Slm accumulates products of C_L and C_M, etc.

(2) The FOR loop from 240 to 400 inputs the tunnel measurements of incidence, lift and pitching moment. After calculating tunnel values of C_L and C_M, corrected values are found at 300 to 320. Lines 330 to 390 accumulate regression summations.

(3) Corrected values are printed at 420 to 480 and then the slopes and intercepts of the best straight line fits to $C_L \sim \alpha$ and $C_M \sim C_L$ are calculated and printed at 490 to 570. The PRINT USING statement to control format and layout is used in this program in two forms: (a) line 460 is controlled by a separate IMAGE statement in line 230; (b) lines 530 to 570 are controlled by their own internal, 'tailor made' image instructions.

(4) In the right-hand column, it can be seen that the centre of pressure is forward of the aerodynamic centre at negative lift, and that it moves forwards as incidence increases from -4 to -2. At positive lift, it lies behind the aerodynamic centre and moves forwards towards that point as incidence increases.

Example 5.2   JOUVELPRE: the calculation of fluid speeds and pressure coefficients on the surface of a Joukowski aerofoil with circulation at zero incidence

This program allows the operator to choose the position of the centre of a circle in the z plane which the Joukowski equation, $Z = z + 1/z^2$, will transform into an aerofoil in the Z plane. Coordinates of 36 points on the aerofoil are found by transforming points at 10 degree intervals from the circle. After the circulation has been input, the program evaluates the speeds and pressure coefficients on the aerofoil. Speed is calculated using Equation (5.8); $Q_a = q_c/M$ where Q_a is the fluid speed on the aerofoil, q_c is the fluid speed on the circle, and $M = |1 - 1/z^2|$; clearly, precautions must be taken to deal with possible zero values of M.

```
10     PRINT "PLEASE INPUT COORDS OF CENTRE OF CIRCLE"
20     PRINT "THE X COORD SHOULD BE NEGATIVE OR ZERO ";
30     INPUT G,H
40     IF G>0 THEN 20
50     PRINT G,H
60     PRINT
70     PRINT "PLEASE INPUT THE NON DIMENSIONAL CIRCULATION, Gam/(4 PI Ua) ";
80     INPUT C
90     PRINT C
100    PRINT
110    PRINT "        CIRCLE                                AEROFOIL "
120    PRINT "Theta    Velocity            Coordinates        Velocity    Pres
 Coeff"
130    R=SQR((1-G)*(1-G)+H*H)
140    FOR I=0 TO 36
150      Th=I*PI/18
160      Xc=G+R*COS(Th)
170      Yc=H+R*SIN(Th)
180      Qc=ABS(-2*SIN(Th)-2*C)
190      R2=Xc*Xc+Yc*Yc
200      Xa=Xc*(1+1/R2)
210      Ya=Yc*(1-1/R2)
220      Re=Xc*Xc-Yc*Yc
230      Im=2*Xc*Yc
240      D=Re*Re+Im*Im
250      Rr=1-Re/D
260      Ii=Im/D
270      M=SQR(Rr*Rr+Ii*Ii)
280      IF ABS(M)<.0001 THEN 330
290      Qa=Qc/M
300      Cp=1-Qa*Qa
310      PRINT USING "DDD,6X,D.DDD,12X,4(DDDD.DDD,4X)";I*10,Qc,Xa,Ya,Qa,Cp
320      GOTO 340
330      PRINT USING "DDD,6X,D.DDD,12X,2(DDDD.DDD,4X),24A";I*10,Qc,Xa,Ya,"  WARN
ING: M IS SMALL"
340    NEXT I
350    END
```

```
RUN
PLEASE INPUT COORDS OF CENTRE OF CIRCLE
THE X COORD SHOULD BE NEGATIVE OR ZERO  0          0

PLEASE INPUT THE NON DIMENSIONAL CIRCULATION, Gam/(4 PI Ua)   0
```

	CIRCLE			AEROFOIL	
Theta	Velocity	Coordinates		Velocity	Pres Coeff
0	0.000	2.000	0.000	WARNING: M IS SMALL	
30	1.000	1.732	0.000	1.000	-0.000
60	1.732	1.000	0.000	1.000	0.000
90	2.000	0.000	0.000	1.000	0.000
120	1.732	-1.000	0.000	1.000	0.000
150	1.000	-1.732	0.000	1.000	0.000
180	0.000	-2.000	0.000	WARNING: M IS SMALL	
210	1.000	-1.732	0.000	1.000	0.000
240	1.732	-1.000	0.000	1.000	0.000
270	2.000	-0.000	0.000	1.000	0.000
300	1.732	1.000	0.000	1.000	0.000
330	1.000	1.732	0.000	1.000	0.000
360	0.000	2.000	0.000	WARNING: M IS SMALL	

```
RUN
PLEASE INPUT COORDS OF CENTRE OF CIRCLE
THE X COORD SHOULD BE NEGATIVE OR ZERO  -.2          .1

PLEASE INPUT THE NON DIMENSIONAL CIRCULATION, Gam/(4 PI Ua)   .8
```

	CIRCLE			AEROFOIL	
Theta	Velocity	Coordinates		Velocity	Pres Coeff
0	1.600	1.990	.002	8.113	-64.815
10	1.947	1.909	.020	3.343	-10.173
20	2.284	1.756	.059	2.501	-5.253
30	2.600	1.543	.119	2.205	-3.862
40	2.886	1.284	.194	2.095	-3.388
50	3.132	.992	.279	2.071	-3.290
60	3.332	.676	.364	2.096	-3.394
70	3.479	.348	.443	2.151	-3.626
80	3.570	.015	.508	2.224	-3.948
90	3.600	-.315	.555	2.311	-4.342
100	3.570	-.634	.580	2.408	-4.797
110	3.479	-.935	.580	2.512	-5.310
120	3.332	-1.214	.557	2.624	-5.888
130	3.132	-1.462	.510	2.747	-6.546
140	2.886	-1.677	.442	2.883	-7.310
150	2.600	-1.853	.358	3.034	-8.207
160	2.284	-1.986	.260	3.193	-9.195
170	1.947	-2.073	.156	3.301	-9.895
180	1.600	-2.113	.050	3.165	-9.016
190	1.253	-2.103	-.053	2.528	-5.390
200	.916	-2.043	-.145	1.600	-1.560
210	.600	-1.935	-.223	.841	.293
220	.314	-1.777	-.281	.353	.875
230	.068	-1.573	-.316	.063	.996
240	.132	-1.326	-.328	.103	.989
250	.279	-1.037	-.314	.191	.964
260	.370	-.713	-.279	.226	.949
270	.400	-.359	-.227	.227	.949
280	.370	.017	-.165	.200	.960
290	.279	.403	-.101	.150	.978
300	.132	.785	-.045	.074	.995
310	.068	1.145	-.005	.042	.998
320	.314	1.462	.016	.228	.948
330	.600	1.719	.020	.575	.670
340	.916	1.897	.011	1.415	-1.002
350	1.253	1.988	.002	5.633	-30.729
360	1.600	1.990	.002	8.113	-64.815

Program notes

(1) The non-dimensional circulation, C, referred to in line 70 is Ga/(4 × PI × Ua) where Ga is dimensional circulation (positive clockwise), U is freestream speed and a is circle radius. Arcsin (−C) gives the angular positions of the stagnation points on the circle circumference. Line 130 calculates the circle radius, R, to ensure that it passes through the transformation singular point at $z = 1$.

(2) The coordinates of points on the circle are found at 10° intervals (lines 140 to 170), with circle surface speed calculated at 180. Aerofoil coordinates are found in lines 190 to 210. Lines 220 to 270 find the value of $M = |1 - 1/z^2|$; Re and Im are the real and imaginary parts of z^2 and Rr and Ii are the real and imaginary parts of $(1 - 1/z^2)$. Line 290 calculates the aerofoil surface speed, Q_a, and 300 finds the pressure coefficient; these and other items are printed at 310.

(3) If M is zero, Q_a may be zero, finite and non-zero or infinitely large depending on aerofoil geometry and the circulation present; rather than writing a separate segment of program to deal with all possible cases, a WARNING is given to the operator at line 330 when M is less than 0.0001.

(4) Lines 310 and 330 use PRINT USING for controlling format and layout.

(5) The first RUN shows that, with the circle centre at (0,0) and with zero circulation, the program calculates speeds and pressures over the surface of a flat plate at zero incidence; these are, as expected, the freestream values. To save space, the output is given at 30° intervals. Note the appearance of the WARNING at 0, 180 and 360 arising from the zero value of M at these points.

(6) The second RUN is for a cambered aerofoil with non-zero thickness and circulation. Note:

(1) The very low pressure at 0° which corresponds to a point on the aerofoil very close to the trailing edge where C_p is infinitely large.
(2) The generally low pressures on the upper surface and the generally high pressures on the lower surface, giving rise to the overall lift force, $\rho U \Gamma$.
(3) The stagnation points close to 230 and 310; both points are on the aerofoil lower surface and neither is close to the leading or trailing edge.

Example 5.3   SOURPANL: the representation of a cylinder by a regular polygon of source panels

This program attempts to reproduce the flow of a uniform stream around a cylinder of unit radius, by replacing the cylinder by a set of source panels forming a regular eight-sided polygon, as shown in Figure 5.10.

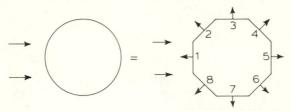

Figure 5.10 Cylinder replaced by eight sided source polygon

The source density strengths of each panel: λ_1, λ_2, . . . λ_8 are initially unknown and the program calculates the 8×8 matrix of coefficients of λ_i in the set of eight simultaneous linear Equations (5.18). These equations are then solved for the eight values of λ_i, using a matrix inversion. To find the coefficients, consider, in Figure 5.11, the velocity induced at the control (centre) points of panel i by panel j $(i \neq j)$.

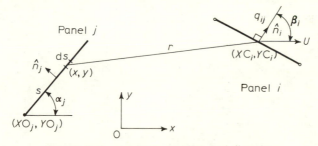

Figure 5.11 Panel relative positions and distances

For $i \neq j$, the velocity component perpendicular to panel i due to a small source element of panel j at (x, y) is dq_{ij} where

$$dq_{ij} = \frac{\partial}{\partial n_i} \left(\frac{\lambda_j ds}{2\pi} \right) \ln r = \frac{\lambda_j ds}{2\pi} \frac{1}{r} \frac{\partial r}{\partial n_i}$$

$$= \frac{\lambda_j ds}{2\pi r} \left[\frac{\partial x_i}{\partial n_i} \frac{(xc_i - x)}{r} + \frac{\partial y_i}{\partial n_i} \frac{(yc_i - y)}{r} \right]$$

where $\partial x_i / \partial n_i$ and $\partial y_i / \partial n_i$ are cosines of the angles between $\hat{n}_i$ and the axes.

Representing the angle between $0x$ and the line j by α_j, and the angle between $0x$ and the outward normal to line i by β_i, the total velocity component perpendicular to panel i induced by panel j is

$$q_{ij} = \frac{\lambda_j}{2\pi} \int_{S=0}^{L} \left[\frac{(xc_i - x) \cos \beta_i + (yc_i - y) \sin \beta_i}{(xc_i - x)^2 + (yc_i - y)^2} \right] ds$$

$$= \frac{\lambda_j}{2\pi} qq_{ij}$$

where qq_{ij} represents the integral, $x = X0_j + s \cos \alpha_j$, $y = Y0_j + s \sin \alpha_j$ and $L = $ length of panel j. The integral may be evaluated in terms of ln and arctan functions. For $i = j$, $qq_{ii} = \pi$. The set of eight Equations (5.18) is now

$$2\pi U \cos \beta_i + \sum_{j=1}^{8} \lambda_j qq_{ij} = 0$$

for $i = 1$ to 8. These equations are solved for the eight source panel strengths by matrix inversion.

```
10      DIM X0(8),Y0(8),Alf(8),Bet(8),Xc(8),Yc(8),Qq(8,8),A(8,16),C(8),Invm(8,8)
20      N=8
30      PRINT "THE CYLINDER IS REPRESENTED BY A POLYGON OF SOURCE PANELS WITH ";N;
" SIDES"
40      REM
50      PRINT
60      PRINT."    PANEL        X0        Y0        ALPHA       BETA        XC
    YC    "
70      L=2*SIN(PI/N)
80      FOR I=1 TO N
90          X0(I)=-COS((3*PI-2*PI*I)/N)
100         Y0(I)=-SIN((3*PI-2*PI*I)/N)
110         Alf(I)=PI/2-(I-1)*2*PI/N
120         Bet(I)=PI-(I-1)*2*PI/N
130         Xc(I)=COS(PI/N)*COS(PI-(I-1)*2*PI/N)
140         Yc(I)=COS(PI/N)*SIN(PI-(I-1)*2*PI/N)
150         PRINT USING "DDDD.DDD,3X";I,X0(I),Y0(I),Alf(I)*180/PI,Bet(I)*180/PI,Xc(I
),Yc(I)
160     NEXT I
170     PRINT
180     PRINT "MATRIX OF COEFFICIENTS OF LAMDA IN EQUATIONS (5.18) IS:"
190     PRINT
200     IMAGE D.DDDD,2X,#
210     FOR I=1 TO N
220       FOR J=1 TO N
230         IF I=J THEN 310
240         E=((Xc(I)-X0(J))*COS(Alf(J))+(Yc(I)-Y0(J))*SIN(Alf(J)))*2
250         F=(Xc(I)-X0(J))^2+(Yc(I)-Y0(J))^2
260         D=SQR(F-E*E/4)
270         U=(Xc(I)-X0(J))*COS(Bet(I))+(Yc(I)-Y0(J))*SIN(Bet(I))
280         V=COS(Alf(J)-Bet(I))
290         Qq(I,J)=-V/2*LOG(((L-E/2)^2+D*D)/F)+(U-E*V/2)/D*ATN(L*D/(F-E*L/2))
300         GOTO 320
310         Qq(I,J)=PI
320         PRINT USING 200:Qq(I,J)
330       NEXT J
340     PRINT
```

```
350    NEXT I
360    D2=1
370    FOR I=1 TO N
380      FOR J=1 TO N
390        A(I,J)=Qq(I,J)
400        IF I=J THEN 430
410        A(I,J+N)=0
420        GOTO 440
430        A(I,J+N)=1
440      NEXT J
450      C(I)=I
460    NEXT I
470    FOR I=1 TO N
480      P=0
490      FOR J=1 TO N
500        IF P>ABS(A(I,J)) THEN 530
510        P=ABS(A(I,J))
520        R=J
530      NEXT J
540      IF I=N THEN 650
550      IF R=I THEN 650
560      D2=D2*(-1)
570      FOR J=1 TO 2*N
580        T=A(I,J)
590        A(I,J)=A(R,J)
600        A(R,J)=T
610      NEXT J
620      T=C(R)
630      C(R)=C(I)
640      C(I)=T
650      D=A(I,I)
660      D2=D2*D
670      FOR J=1 TO 2*N
680        A(I,J)=A(I,J)/D
690      NEXT J
700      FOR I1=1 TO N
710        IF I1=I THEN 760
720        D=A(I1,I)
730        FOR J=1 TO 2*N
740          A(I1,J)=A(I1,J)-D*A(I,J)
750        NEXT J
760      NEXT I1
770    NEXT I
780    PRINT
790    PRINT "INVERSE MATRIX IS "
800    PRINT
810    FOR I=1 TO N
820      FOR J=1 TO N
830        Invm(I,J)=A(I,J+N)
840        PRINT USING 200;Invm(I,J)
850      NEXT J
860      PRINT
870    NEXT I
880    PRINT
890    PRINT "SOURCE PANEL STRENGTHS/(2 PI U) ARE:"
900    PRINT
910    FOR I=1 TO N
920      L=0
930      FOR J=1 TO N
940        L=L-Invm(I,J)*COS(Bet(J))
950      NEXT J
960      PRINT USING 200;L
970    NEXT I
980    END
```

RUN

RUN
THE CYLINDER IS REPRESENTED BY A POLYGON OF SOURCE PANELS WITH 8 SIDES

PANEL	XO	YO	ALPHA	BETA	XC	YC
1.000	-.924	-.383	90.000	180.000	-.924	0.000
2.000	-.924	.383	45.000	135.000	-.653	.653
3.000	-.383	.924	0.000	90.000	0.000	.924
4.000	.383	.924	-45.000	45.000	.653	.653
5.000	.924	.383	-90.000	0.000	.924	0.000
6.000	.924	-.383	-135.000	-45.000	.653	-.653
7.000	.383	-.924	-180.000	-90.000	0.000	-.924
8.000	-.383	-.924	-225.000	-135.000	-.653	-.653

```
MATRIX OF COEFFICIENTS OF LAMDA IN EQUATIONS (5.18) IS:

3.1416    .3528     .4018     .4074     .4084     .4074     .4018     .3528
 .3528   3.1416     .3528     .4018     .4074     .4084     .4074     .4018
 .4018    .3528    3.1416     .3528     .4018     .4074     .4084     .4074
 .4074    .4018     .3528    3.1416     .3528     .4018     .4074     .4084
 .4084    .4074     .4018     .3528    3.1416     .3528     .4018     .4074
 .4074    .4084     .4074     .4018     .3528    3.1416     .3528     .4018
 .4018    .4074     .4084     .4074     .4018     .3528    3.1416     .3528
 .3528    .4018     .4074     .4084     .4074     .4018     .3528    3.1416

INVERSE MATRIX IS

 .3395   -.0192    -.0256    -.0265    -.0267    -.0265    -.0256    -.0192
-.0192    .3395    -.0192    -.0256    -.0265    -.0267    -.0265    -.0256
-.0256   -.0192     .3395    -.0192    -.0256    -.0265    -.0267    -.0265
-.0265   -.0256    -.0192     .3395    -.0192    -.0256    -.0265    -.0267
-.0267   -.0265    -.0256    -.0192     .3395    -.0192    -.0256    -.0265
-.0265   -.0267    -.0265    -.0256    -.0192     .3395    -.0192    -.0256
-.0256   -.0265    -.0267    -.0265    -.0256    -.0192     .3395    -.0192
-.0192   -.0256    -.0265    -.0267    -.0265    -.0256    -.0192     .3395

SOURCE PANEL STRENGTHS/(2 PI U) ARE:

 .3765    .2662    -.0000    -.2662    -.3765    -.2662   0.0000     .2662
```

Program notes

(1) Line 10 declares dimensions of the arrays which will store data during the calculation. X0 and Y0, XC and YC store coordinates of the initial points and centre control points of the eight panels; Alf and Bet store the directions of the panel lines and the directions of the outward normals respectively (see Figure 5.11). Qq stores the matrix of coefficients of the λ_i and Invm stores its inverse. A and C are supplementary arrays used during inversion.

(2) Lines 60 to 160 calculate, store and print geometric information on the panels, i.e. values of X0, Y0, XC, YC, α_i and β_i are found.

(3) Lines 210 to 350 calculate, store and print Qq, the elements of the matrix of coefficients of λ_i. The equations listed in the introduction to this program are used to find Qq, distinguishing between the cases $i \neq j$ (240 to 290) and $i = j$ (310).

(4) The matrix is inverted 'longhand' by statements 360 to 770 using a form of Gaussian elimination; the result is printed by lines 790 to 870. Finally, the product of this inverse matrix and the matrix of cos β elements is evaluated and printed by lines 910 to 970.

(5) The IMAGE statement at line 200 controls the format of the PRINT USING statement at lines 320, 840 and 960; the # suppresses the normal carriage return/linefeed sequence which follows a PRINT statement.

(6) Note that the RUN results show that the total source strength is zero.

(7) The program may easily be altered to cater for polygons of source panels with sides other than eight; the only two lines requiring amendment are 10 and 20. Below is shown a RUN for N = 12, with all output suppressed except panel strengths:

RUN
THE CYLINDER IS REPRESENTED BY A POLYGON OF
SOURCE PANELS WITH 12 SIDES

SOURCE PANEL STRENGTHS/(2PI U) ARE:

.3562   .3084   .1781   0.0000   −.1781   −.3084   −.3562
−.3084   −.1781   0.0000   .1781   .3084

Example 5.4   THINAERO: the use of thin aerofoil theory to determine the aerodynamic properties of aerofoil sections with prescribed camber lines

This program uses thin aerofoil theory results to find the aerodynamic characteristics of NACA four digit series wing sections which have camber lines formed from two parabolic arcs, both tangential to the aerofoil chord line at the position of maximum camber.

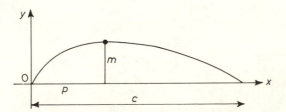

Figure 5.12 Aerofoil camber line formed by two parabolas

Using a set of axes with origin at the aerofoil leading edge and with $0x$ along the chord line, the equations of these parabolas are

$$y = m(2px - x^2)/p^2 \qquad \text{for } O \leqslant x \leqslant p$$
$$y = m[c(c - 2p) + 2px - x^2]/(c - p)^2 \quad \text{for } p \leqslant x \leqslant c$$

where m is the maximum camber line ordinate and p is the chordwise position of the maximum ordinate.

The operator inputs selected values of m and p and the program integrates Equations (5.29) and (5.30) numerically to determine the Fourier coefficients A_0, A_1 and A_2. Aerodynamic properties of the aerofoil are then printed, together with a table of values of C_L and C_M.

```
10      PRINT "PLEASE INPUT THE MAXIMUM CAMBER LINE ORDINATE AND ITS CHORDWISE"
20      PRINT "POSITION AS A FRACTION OF AEROFOIL CHORD ";
30      INPUT M,P
40      PRINT M,P
50      PRINT
60      FOR N=0 TO 2
70        S=0
80        FOR I=1 TO 72
90          Th=(I-.5)*PI/72
100         X=(1-COS(Th))/2
110         GOSUB Camber
120         S=S+Dy*COS(N*Th)*PI/72
130       NEXT I
140       IF N>0 THEN 170
150       A(0)=S/PI
160       GOTO 180
170       A(N)=S*2/PI
180     NEXT N
190     PRINT "A(N) COEFFICIENTS ARE:- ";A(0);A(1);A(2)
200     PRINT
210     PRINT "ZERO LIFT ANGLE = ";(2*A(0)-A(1))*90/PI;" DEG"
220     PRINT "QUARTER CHORD PITCHING MOMENT COEFFICIENT = ";PI*(A(2)-A(1))/4
230     PRINT
240     PRINT "INCIDENCE         CL                 CM(LE)"
250     FOR Alfa=-4 TO 12 STEP 2
260       PRINT Alfa,2*PI*PI/180*Alfa-PI*(2*A(0)-A(1)),-(Alfa*PI/180-A(0)+A(1)-A(2
)/2)*PI/2
270     NEXT Alfa
280     GOTO 340
290 Camber:   IF X>P THEN 320
300             Dy=M*(2*P-2*X)/(P^2)
310             GOTO 330
320             Dy=M*(2*P-2*X)/((1-P)^2)
330     RETURN
340     END
```

```
RUN
PLEASE INPUT THE MAXIMUM CAMBER LINE ORDINATE AND ITS CHORDWISE
POSITION AS A FRACTION OF AEROFOIL CHORD  0        .2

A(N) COEFFICIENTS ARE:-   0  0  0

ZERO LIFT ANGLE =   0  DEG
QUARTER CHORD PITCHING MOMENT COEFFICIENT =   0
```

INCIDENCE	CL	CM(LE)
-4	-.438649084493	.109662271123
-2	-.219324542246	.0548311355616
0	0	0
2	.219324542246	-.0548311355616
4	.438649084493	-.109662271123
6	.657973626739	-.164493406685
8	.877298168986	-.219324542246
10	1.09662271123	-.274155677808
12	1.31594725348	-.32898681337

```
RUN
PLEASE INPUT THE MAXIMUM CAMBER LINE ORDINATE AND ITS CHORDWISE
POSITION AS A FRACTION OF AEROFOIL CHORD  .04      .2

A(N) COEFFICIENTS ARE:-   .0352052299699  .195985594082  .101857901711
```

```
ZERO LIFT ANGLE = -3.59746259906  DEG
QUARTER CHORD PITCHING MOMENT COEFFICIENT = -.0739277167126
```

INCIDENCE	CL	CM(LE)
-4	-.0441431655992	-.0628919253128
-2	.175181376647	-.117723060874
0	.394505918894	-.172554196436
2	.61383046114	-.227385331998
4	.833155003387	-.282216467559
6	1.05247954563	-.337047603121
8	1.27180408788	-.391878738682
10	1.49112863013	-.446709874244
12	1.71045317237	-.501541009806

Program notes

(1) Lines 10 to 40 request the values of the percentage camber and the maximum camber position.

(2) Lines 60 to 180 contain a FOR loop which evaluates, for N = 0, 1 and 2, the Fourier coefficients A(N). These coefficients are computed by numerical integration of Equations (5.29) and (5.30), the range of integration, $0 \le \theta \le \pi$, being subdivided into 72 intervals, each contributing to the integration sum S through the FOR loop between lines 80 and 130. Lines 140 to 160 arrange for the case N = 0 to be treated differently from the other two cases in the evaluation of A(N).

(3) The calculation of the camber line gradient dy/dx is accomplished through a SUBROUTINE labelled Camber. The subroutine is called at line 110 and the program then jumps to 290 where the subroutine commences; it returns from 330 to 120 with the current value of Dy, the required gradient.

(4) Lines 190 to 270 print output data, including a table of values of C_L and $C_{M_{LE}}$ at two-degree intervals of incidence from −4 to +12.

PROBLEMS

(5.1) Write a program which inputs distance from the leading edge of a symmetric aerofoil section at incidence α, and which then calculates the pressure difference across the aerofoil at that point. The vorticity distribution may be assumed to be given by

$$\gamma = 2U\alpha \left(\frac{1 + \cos \theta}{\sin \theta}\right)$$

$$x = \frac{c}{2} (1 - \cos \theta)$$

Make special provision for the leading edge and, if you think it necessary, for the trailing edge too.

Divide the aerofoil chord into N sections and carry out a numerical integration of the lift forces and pitching moments generated at each section, assuming that the pressure difference is constant, at the centre point value, across each section. Print the results and compare them with the values derived from analytical integration.

(5.2) Write a program which inputs incidence and flap deflection angle of a symmetric aerofoil section with flap, and which calculates C_L and C_M. The flap extends over a fraction E of the chord as shown in Figure 5.9. Then extend the program to tabulate either C_L or C_M for a range of incidences and flap angles.

(5.3) Write a program which tabulates (and if graphics are available, plots) coordinates of a streamline with a specified value of the stream function, in the flow around a specified Joukowski aerofoil at zero incidence.

(5.4) Extend Example 5.2 to calculate the fluid speed and pressure coefficient at any point on the surface of a Joukowski aerofoil at non-zero incidence. Start with zero circulation and then modify the program to cater for general incidence and circulation.

(5.5) The ordinates of a 20% thickness/chord ratio symmetrical aerofoil section are given by

$$\pm y = 0.34 \sqrt{x} - 0.18x - 0.5x^2 + 0.34x^3$$

If this aerofoil may be represented by nine doublets at $x = 0.1(0.1)0.9$, write a program to find suitable strengths for these doublets (try different control point positions). Then find velocities and pressure coefficients at your selected control points.

(5.6) Write a program, similar to Example 5.1, which will input wind tunnel readings of a model wing incidence, lift and drag forces, add the corrections as detailed below and tabulate corrected values of incidence, lift and drag coefficient, together with zero lift drag coefficient and the slope of the $C_D \sim C_L$ line. Corrections are

$$\Delta \alpha = \delta \frac{S}{n} C_L \text{ rad}$$

$$\Delta C_D = C_L \Delta \alpha$$

where δ is a tunnel shape factor (typical value 0.12), A is a tunnel working section cross sectional area and S is the model wing area.

Chapter 6

Finite wing theory

ESSENTIAL THEORY

6.1 Introduction and definitions

A wing is a lifting surface of finite span, which is normally symmetrical about a central plane perpendicular to its span; fluid motion over the wing occurs in spanwise as well as in a chordwise direction.

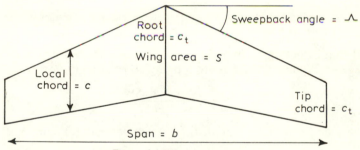

Figure 6.1 Wing geometry

Standard mean chord = $\bar{c}$ = S/b, aspect ratio = A = $b/\bar{c}$ = b^2/S, taper ratio = tip chord/root chord = λ.

6.2 Vortex theory

6.2.1 Helmholz vortex theorems

The following results, known as Helmholz vortex theorems, apply to a free vortex line or filament:

(1) The strength of a vortex filament is constant along its length.

(2) A vortex filament cannot end in a fluid; it must form a closed loop or extend to the boundaries of the fluid.

(3) In the absence of external torques, a fluid which is initially irrotational will remain irrotational.

6.2.2   Biot Savart law

The velocity v induced at a general point P by a small element (of length ds at 0) of a vortex of strength Γ, is given by

$$v = \frac{\Gamma}{4\pi r} \sin \theta \, \mathrm{d}s \qquad (6.1)$$

where r is the distance OP and θ is the angle between the direction of the element and the direction OP; v is in the direction perpendicular to both OP and the element.

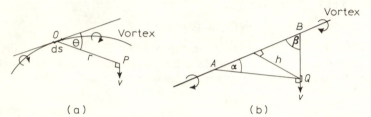

(a)   (b)

Figure 6.2 Velocity induced by (a) an element, (b) a straight line segment of a vortex

From Equation (6.1), it can be shown that the velocity induced at general point Q by a finite length AB of straight vortex is

$$v = \frac{\Gamma (\cos \alpha + \cos \beta)}{4\pi h} \qquad (6.2)$$

where angles α and β, and distance h are defined in Figure 6.2(b).

6.3   Lifting line theory

In an analysis of its lifting properties, a wing may be considered equivalent to a vortex running across the span along the quarter chord line, i.e. the wing may be replaced by a 'bound vortex' or

Figure 6.3 General wing vortex system

'lifting line'. As explained in Section 5.2, a constant strength bound vortex will produce a uniform spanwise lift distribution, but this bound vortex cannot, by Helmholz' theorem, end at wing tips; it must continue in the downstream direction and form a closed rectangular circuit with the starting vortex.

Around a general wing, the lift and the corresponding bound vortex strength is not uniform across the span, and the vortex system is shown in Figure 6.3. To satisfy Helmholz, a small vortex is trailed from the wing wherever the bound vortex strength changes, and the integrated effect of the resulting trailing vortex sheet is to produce a downflow between the wing tips ahead, across the span and to the rear of the wing.

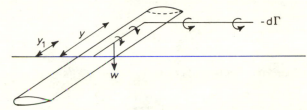

Figure 6.4 Downwash w at station y_1 resulting from a vortex trailed from y

At a point on the wing quarter chord line at distance y_1 from the wing plane of symmetry (y is positive on the starboard side), the downwash velocity w is

$$w = -\frac{1}{4\pi} \int_{-b/2}^{+b/2} \frac{\frac{d\Gamma}{dy}}{(y - y_1)} \, dy \qquad (6.3)$$

and the local section incidence α_e (effective incidence) is related to freestream incidence α (geometric incidence) and downwash angle ϵ by

$$\alpha_e = \alpha - \epsilon \qquad (6.4)$$

where $\epsilon = w/U$. Total lift force component perpendicular to the freestream is

$$L = \int_{-b/2}^{+b/2} \rho U \Gamma \, dy \qquad (6.5)$$

and the total induced drag component parallel to the freestream is

$$D_i = \int_{-b/2}^{+b/2} \rho w \Gamma \, dy \qquad (6.6)$$

Lift, drag and downwash may be calculated from the above equations if the variation of bound vortex strength Γ with spanwise distance y is specified. It is usual to express Γ as a function of y using an angle ϕ as a position parameter, where

$$y = -\frac{b}{2} \cos \phi \qquad \text{with } 0 \le \phi \le \pi \qquad (6.7)$$

and then

$$\Gamma = f(\phi) \qquad (6.8)$$

6.3.1 *Elliptic distribution of bound vortex strength*

If

$$\Gamma = \Gamma_0 \sin \phi \qquad (6.9)$$

then Equations (6.7) and (6.9) define an elliptic spanwise circulation distribution with centreline strength Γ_0. Downwash, from Equation (6.3), is

$$w = \Gamma_0/2b \qquad (6.10)$$

i.e. downwash is constant across the span. Lift, from Equation (6.5), is

$$C_L = \frac{\Gamma_0 \pi b}{2US} \qquad (6.11)$$

and induced drag, from Equation (6.6), is

$$C_{D_i} = \frac{\Gamma_0^2 \pi}{4U^2 S} = \frac{C_L^2}{\pi A} \qquad (6.12)$$

The wing downwash angle, from Equations (6.4) and (6.10), is

$$\epsilon = w/U = \frac{\Gamma_0}{2Ub} = \frac{C_L}{\pi A} \qquad (6.13)$$

and, for an untwisted wing, the local effective incidence, from Equation (6.4), is

$$\alpha_e = \alpha = \frac{C_L}{\pi A} \qquad (6.14)$$

Relating C_L to this effective incidence through the two-dimensional lift curve slope a_∞ gives

$$C_L = a_\infty \alpha_e = \frac{a_\infty}{1 + \dfrac{a_\infty}{\pi A}} \tag{6.15}$$

i.e. the lift curve slope is a function of aspect ratio.

Expressing Equation (6.4) in terms of local chord c, local geometric incidence α and position parameter ϕ gives

$$\mu\alpha = \frac{\Gamma_0}{2Ub} \sin\phi \left(1 + \frac{\mu}{\sin\phi}\right) \tag{6.16}$$

where $\mu = a_\infty c/4b$. This is the elliptic loading form of the general monoplane equation (see Equation (6.23)). If the wing is untwisted, then α is constant and the monoplane equation gives

$$c = \frac{4b}{\pi A} \sin\phi \tag{6.17}$$

showing that, for elliptic loading with an untwisted wing, the planform should be elliptic with centreline chord $4b/\pi A$. The mean chord is of course b/A. If the wing is twisted, so that geometric incidence varies across the span, then the monoplane Equation (6.6) tells how chord must be distributed in terms of ϕ in order to maintain elliptic loading.

6.3.2 General distribution of spanwise loading

A general spanwise distribution of circulation Γ may be expressed as a Fourier series in the position parameter ϕ, using only sine terms in order to obtain zero loading at the wing tips and omitting even harmonic terms to obtain symmetry about the wing central plane. Then, as above, $y = -b/2 \cos\phi$, and now:

$$\Gamma = 2Ub \sum_{n=1}^{\infty} A_n \sin n\phi \quad (n \text{ odd}) \tag{6.18}$$

Downwash, from Equation (6.3):

$$w = U \sum_{n=1}^{\infty} \frac{nA_n \sin n\phi}{\sin\phi} \quad (n \text{ odd}) \tag{6.19}$$

Total wing lift, from Equation (6.5):

$$C_L = \pi A A_1 \qquad (6.20)$$

This agrees with the elliptic loading case, Equation (6.11), when $A_1 = \Gamma_0/2Ub$.

Total induced drag, from Equation (6.6):

$$C_{D_i} = \frac{C_L^2}{\pi A} (1 + \delta) \qquad (6.21)$$

where

$$\delta = \frac{1}{A_1^2} (3A_3^2 + 5A_5^2 + 7A_7^2 + \ldots) \geqslant 0 \qquad (6.22)$$

Minimum induced drag occurs with an elliptic loading, when $\delta = 0$.

The monoplane equation

The monoplane equation for a general loading is obtained from Equation (6.4):

$$\mu\alpha \sin \phi = \sum_{1}^{\infty} A_n \sin n\phi \, (\sin \phi + n\mu) \quad (n \text{ odd}) \quad (6.23)$$

where $\mu = ca_\infty/4b$. If the aerofoil section zero lift angle is α_0, then α is replaced by $(\alpha - \alpha_0)$.

6.4   Lifting surface theory

On a large scale, lifting line theory agrees well with experimental results for unswept, high aspect ratio wings but for swept wings, low aspect ratio wings or for detailed investigations of particular regions of any wing (e.g. the flow near the tips or roots), a more refined method is needed. This is provided by lifting surface theory which distributes vorticity continuously over the surface area of the wing; the boundary condition that there is no velocity component normal to the surface is imposed at the surface.

6.4.1   Vortex lattice method

This is a numerical technique for applying lifting surface ideas. The wing is divided into N small elementary areas, bounded by chord lines parallel to the plane of symmetry and by lines of constant chord fraction running spanwise across the wing as shown in Figure 6.5.

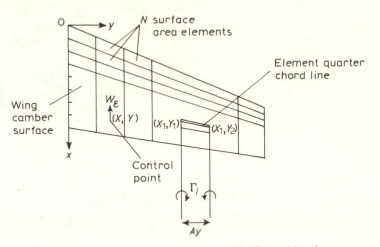

Figure 6.5 Velocity w_i at control point (X, Y) resulting from a horseshoe vortex with vertices at (X_1, Y_1) and (X_2, Y_2)

Element i carries, along its quarter chord line in the wing camber surface, a bound vortex of unknown strength Γ_i, together with two trailing vortices which run from the elementary bound vortex tips to infinity in the direction of the wing streamwise axis (this direction is normally fixed relative to the wing). The total wing vortex system, comprising small horseshoe vortices attached to each area element, is required to induce zero velocity component perpendicular to the wing camber surface at N control points when combined with the freestream; there is one control point in each elementary area placed at the mid spanwise position on the three-quarter chord line.

6.4.2 The plane wing

To calculate velocities induced by the lattice of vortices, an axis system is set up as shown in Figure 6.5. If the wing is assumed to be planar, then the velocity w_i (positive upwards) induced at a general point (X, Y) by a 'horseshoe vortex' comprising:

(1) A bound vortex of strength Γ_i lying between (x_1, y_1) and (x_2, y_2) with $y_1 < y_2$.

(2) Two trailing vortices running from (x_1, y_1) and (x_2, y_2) to 'infinity' in the positive $0x$ direction.

is given by the Biot Savart law as

$$
\begin{aligned}
w_i = \frac{\Gamma_i}{4\pi} \Bigg\{ & \frac{1}{(x_2 - X)(y_1 - Y) - (x_1 - X)(y_2 - Y)} \\
& \times \left[\frac{(x_2 - x_1)(x_1 - X) + (y_2 - y_1)(y_1 - Y)}{\sqrt{(x_1 - X)^2 + (y_1 - Y)^2}} \right. \\
& \left. - \frac{(x_2 - x_1)(x_2 - X) + (y_2 - y_1)(y_2 - Y)}{\sqrt{(x_2 - X)^2 + (y_2 - Y)^2}} \right] \\
& + \frac{1}{(y_1 - Y)} \left[1 - \frac{(x_1 - X)}{\sqrt{(x_1 - X)^2 + (y_1 - Y)^2}} \right] \\
& - \frac{1}{(y_2 - Y)} \left[1 - \frac{(x_2 - X)}{\sqrt{(x_2 - X)^2 + (y_2 - Y)^2}} \right] \Bigg\}
\end{aligned}
$$

(6.24)

Contributions from all the vortices are added at each control point, so that for a planar wing at a small incidence angle α:

$$
\sum_{i=1}^{N} w_i + U\alpha = 0 \qquad (N \text{ Equations}) \quad (6.25)
$$

in order that fluid velocity perpendicular to the wing plane should be zero at every control point. The N Equations (6.25) together with (6.24) are solved for the N unknown vortex strengths Γ_i in terms of the freestream speed U, the wing incidence α and the wing dimensions. The lift per unit span generated by each area element is $\rho U \Gamma_i$, and the total wing lift is

$$
L = \sum_{i=1}^{N} \rho U \Gamma_i \Delta y_i \qquad (6.26)
$$

where Δy_i is the width of the area element containing bound vortex Γ_i. The summation extends over all N surface elements of the wing. To estimate the local lift per unit span at spanwise position y_1, vortex strengths at y_1 are summed from leading edge to trailing edge.

6.5 Subsonic compressibility effects

On unswept wings, the Prandtl–Glauert factor, $1/\sqrt{1 - M^2}$, may be applied to all pressure dependent quantities so that

$$C_L = a\alpha/\sqrt{1 - M^2} \qquad (6.27)$$

where a is the lift curve slope in incompressible conditions. Wing lift curve slope, taking aerofoil lift curve slope in incompressible flow to be 2π, is

$$a(M) = \frac{2\pi}{(1 + 2/A)(1 - M^2)^{1/2}} \qquad (6.28)$$

This expression overestimates $a(M)$ and one (of several) proposed improvements is

$$a(M) = \frac{2\pi}{2/A + (4/A^2 + 1 - M^2)^{1/2}} \qquad \text{for } A \geqslant 2 \quad (6.29)$$

6.6 Slender, delta and swept wings

Wings of very low aspect ratio ($A < 1$) are called slender wings; they are normally highly swept deltas.

6.6.1 Slender delta wings

Pressures and surface velocities on slender deltas with sharp leading edges are constant along radial lines passing through the apex of the wing. At small incidence α and freestream U, the perturbation velocities on upper and lower surfaces at spanwise station y are given by

$$u = \pm U\alpha \frac{y_1}{\sqrt{y_1^2 - y^2}} \tan \epsilon \qquad (6.30)$$

and the lifting pressure difference between upper and lower surfaces is

$$C_p = 4\alpha \frac{y_1}{\sqrt{y_1^2 - y^2}} \tan \epsilon \qquad (6.31)$$

where ϵ is the delta wing's semi-vertex angle and y_1 is the wing semi-span at the chordwise position considered. From these equations, it can be seen that the flow is conical because conditions are constant along lines $y/y_1 =$ constant; velocity and pressure tend to infinitely large values along the wing leading edge.

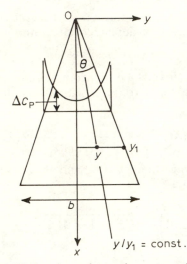

Figure 6.6 Delta wing and spanwise pressure distribution

A chordwise integration of Equation (6.31) shows that the loading across the wing is elliptic, i.e.

$$\frac{dL}{dy} = 2\rho U^2 \alpha \sqrt{(b/2)^2 - y^2} \qquad (6.32)$$

and a further spanwise integration gives

$$C_L = \frac{\text{Lift}}{\tfrac{1}{2}\rho U^2 S} = \frac{\tfrac{1}{4}\rho \pi U^2 b^2 \alpha}{\tfrac{1}{2}\rho U^2 S} = \frac{\pi}{2} A\alpha \qquad (6.33)$$

Lift is dependent on span squared, rather than the usual surface area. Drag

$$C_{D_i} = \frac{C_L \alpha}{2} = C_L^2/\pi A \qquad (6.34)$$

where $A =$ aspect ratio. These results are independent of Mach number at subsonic speeds. Slender wings of general planform are 'quasi-conical' in that the velocities and pressures are expressed by Equations (6.30) and (6.31) of conical theory but the semi-vertex angle ϵ is replaced by the local leading edge slope at the same chordwise station. Integrations of Equation (6.31) in a chordwise and a spanwise direction will give the total lift on the general slender wing.

6.6.2   Delta wings

The preceding slender delta theory assumes that a potential flow is possible resulting in lift proportional to incidence but clearly the infinite values found at the leading edge are not physically tenable. At any non-zero incidence, the flow separates at the sharp leading edge and forms two powerful spiral vortices which lie along two radial lines lying just above and inboard of the leading edges.

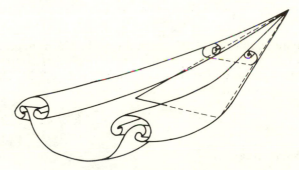

Figure 6.7 Flow over a lifting slender wing

Areas of strong suction pressures are produced on the sections of the surface which are closely affected by these vortices increasing the lift; the total lift may, therefore, be considered to be the sum of a lift resulting from a potential flow and a lift resulting from the vortex flow, and may be represented at incidences below about 20° by

$$C_L = K_p \sin \alpha \cos^2\alpha + K_v \sin^2\alpha \cos \alpha \qquad (6.35)$$

where K_p and K_v are potential flow (derived from lifting surface theory) and vortex flow coefficients, which are functions of aspect ratio (sweepback angle) and Mach number. Figure 6.8 shows the variation of K_p and K_v with aspect ratio at M = 0 (K_v is approximately constant at π).

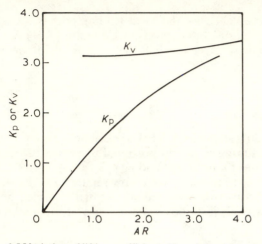

Figure 6.8 Variation of lifting coefficients K_p and K_v with aspect ratio

Subsonic variation of K_p and K_v with Mach number may be obtained by application of the Prandtl–Glauert factor $1/(1 - M^2)^{1/2}$, giving results (for $A = 1$) shown in Figure 7.10. Drag due to lift is $C_L \tan \alpha$ so that

$$C_{D_i} = K_p \sin^2\alpha \cos \alpha + K_v \sin^3\alpha \qquad (6.36)$$

6.6.3   Swept wings

The two-dimensional lift coefficient of an oblique wing with sweepback angle Λ is

$$C_L = \frac{2\pi\alpha \cos \Lambda}{\sqrt{1 - (M \cos \Lambda)^2}} \qquad (6.37)$$

For wings of finite span, lifting surface methods give the results shown in Figure 6.9; lifting line and slender wing theory results are also shown.

6.7   Total wing drag and lift/drag ratio

The total drag of a wing is the sum of viscous drag and lift induced drag. For a high aspect ratio wing using drag Equation (6.21):

$$C_D = C_{D_o} + \frac{kC_L^2}{\pi A} \qquad (6.38)$$

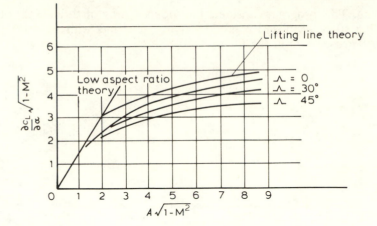

Figure 6.9 Variation of lift curve slope with sweepback angle, Mach number

whereas, for a delta wing using Equation (6.36):

$$C_D = C_{D_o} + K_p \sin^2\alpha \cos\alpha + K_v \sin^3\alpha \qquad (6.39)$$

The lift/drag ratio of a high aspect ratio wing can be shown to be maximum when viscous and induced drags are equal, i.e.

$$C_{D_o} = \frac{kC_L^2}{\pi A} \qquad (6.40)$$

and the maximum lift/drag ratio is

$$(L/D)_{max} = \frac{1}{2} \sqrt{\frac{\pi A}{kC_{D_o}}} \qquad (6.41)$$

A typical value for a wing alone with aspect ratio 6, $k = 1.2$ and $C = 0.008$ is 22; addition of fuselage, tailplane and interference drags of a complete aircraft will reduce $(L/D)_{max}$ to about 12.

WORKED EXAMPLES

Example 6.1 BIRDDRAG: calculation of the induced drag of birds flying in formation

One of the advantages to birds (and aircraft) of flying in echelon formation is that all the birds are positioned to fly in an upwash from their neighbours' vortex systems, thus reducing induced drag. This program considers the induced drag of three birds of wing span 0.8 m and mass 1 kg flying at 10 m/s with separation distances shown in the Figure 6.10.

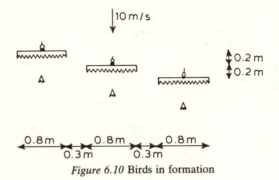

Figure 6.10 Birds in formation

In order to simplify the calculations, it is assumed that circulation is constant across the span of each bird's wing, i.e. spanwise loading is rectangular and the trailing vortex system of each bird is a simple horseshoe; it is also assumed that the induced downwash (or upwash) is constant across the span at the value calculated at the wing centre point.

```
10      Ro=1.225
20      U=10
30      B=.8
40      D1=.2
50      D2=.3
60      M=1
70      Gam=M*9.81/(Ro*U*B)
80        X=0                     ! Calculates the induced drag of an isolated bird
90        Y=0
100       GOSUB 520
110       W0=W
120       Dr0=-Ro*W0*Gam*B
130       W11=W0                  ! Calculates the induced drag of the leading bird
140       X=-D1
150       Y=-(D2+B)
160       GOSUB 520
170       W12=W
180       X=-2*D1
190       Y=-2*(D2+B)
200       GOSUB 520
210       W13=W
220       W1=W11+W12+W13
230       Dr1=-Ro*W1*Gam*B
240       X=D1                    ! Calculates the drag of the middle bird
250       Y=D2+B
260       GOSUB 520
270       W21=W0
280       W22=W0
290       X=-D1
300       Y=-(D2+B)
310       GOSUB 520
320       W23=W
330       W2=W21+W22+W23
340       Dr2=-Ro*W2*Gam*B
350       X=2*D1                  ! Calculates the drag of the trailing bird
```

```
360     Y=2*(D2+B)
370     GOSUB 520
380     W31=W
390     X=D1
400     Y=D2+B
410     GOSUB 520
420     W32=W
430     W33=W0
440     W3=W31+W32+W33
450     Dr3=-Ro*W3*Gam*B
460     IMAGE 36A.D.DDD," Newtons"
470     PRINT USING 460;" INDUCED DRAG OF AN ISOLATED BIRD = ",Dr0
480     PRINT USING 460;" INDUCED DRAG OF LEADING BIRD     = ",Dr1
490     PRINT USING 460;" INDUCED DRAG OF MIDDLE BIRD      = ",Dr2
500     PRINT USING 460;" INDUCED DRAG OF TRAILING BIRD    = ",Dr3
510     GOTO 600
520     G=Gam/(2*PI)
530     Wab=-G*(1+X/SQR(X*X+(Y+B/2)*(Y+B/2)))/(Y+B/2)
540     Wbc=0
550     IF X=0 THEN 570
560     Wbc=-G*((Y+B/2)/SQR(X*X+(Y+B/2)*(Y+B/2))-(Y-B/2)/SQR(X*X+(Y-B/2)*(Y-B/2))
)/X
570     Wcd=G*(1+X/SQR(X*X+(Y-B/2)*(Y-B/2)))/(Y-B/2)
580     W=Wab+Wbc+Wcd
590     RETURN
600     END
```

```
RUN
  INDUCED DRAG OF AN ISOLATED BIRD =   .781 Newtons
  INDUCED DRAG OF LEADING BIRD     =   .665 Newtons
  INDUCED DRAG OF MIDDLE BIRD      =   .543 Newtons
  INDUCED DRAG OF TRAILING BIRD    =   .606 Newtons
```

Program notes

(1) Lines 520 to 590 contain a subroutine which calculates the
velocity W induced by a horseshoe vortex of span B at a general
point (X, Y) relative to Cartesian axes with origin at the mid-point
of the bound vortex and 0x pointing downstream (see Figure 6.11).

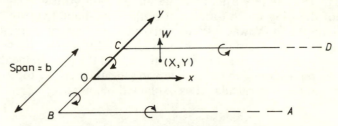

Figure 6.11 Velocity W induced at (X, Y) by a horseshoe vortex

The subroutine is entered with appropriate values of X and Y to
find the induced upwash, W (positive upwards), at the centre of
each bird's lifting line, due to a single horseshoe vortex.

(2) The induced drag of an isolated bird is found in lines 80 to 120.
Lines 130 to 450 calculate the induced drag of the three birds in
formation; the velocities, W_{ij}, induced at bird i by bird j's vortex

are added for each bird and the induced drag is found at lines 230, 340 and 450. The minus sign in these lines and in 120 is a consequence of taking W to be positive upwards.

(3) The comments in lines 80, 130, 240 and 350 are preceded here by ! rather than the usual REM.

(4) Lines 460 to 500 print out results. The following RUN shows that the middle bird comes off best.

Example 6.2   DOWNWASH: investigation of the downwash field behind an aircraft wing in the wing's plane of symmetry

In deciding on the best position for the tailplane of an aircraft, a designer must know the downwash induced behind a wing by its vortex system. In particular, for stability considerations, he needs to know the rate at which downwash angle ϵ changes with wing incidence α. This program calculates this 'downwash derivative' $d\epsilon/d\alpha$ at a series of points in the plane of symmetry behind an elliptically loaded wing of aspect ratio 6 and lift curve slope 5.7/rad.

Reference Equation (6.7), each half of the wing is divided into nine strips of 10° intervals of the position angle ϕ. From the mid-point of each strip, a vortex of strength $\Gamma_0 \cos \phi \, d\phi$ will be trailed downstream, where Γ_0 is the centreline circulation of the elliptically loaded wing and $d\phi = 10°$. A similar strength vortex will be trailed from the symmetric point on the other half wing and the pair of trailing vortices will be linked by a vortex along the span of the wing which forms part of the wing-bound vortex. We calculate the downwash W due to this elementary horseshoe vortex at a point distance Xb behind and Zb above the wing, where b is the span; the contributions from all the nine elementary vortices representing the complete wing are then added together. $d\epsilon/d\alpha$ can then be calculated as explained below.

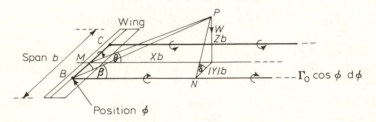

Figure 6.12 Downwash due to an elementary horseshoe vortex

From Equation (6.2), the downwash at point P due to the elementary horseshoe vortex of strength $\Gamma_0 \cos\phi\, d\phi$ shown in Figure 6.12 is

$$W = \frac{\Gamma_0 \cos \phi\, d\phi}{4\pi} \left[\frac{(1 + \cos \beta)\, 2 \cos \delta}{PN} + \frac{2 \cos \gamma \cos \theta}{PM} \right] \quad (1)$$

Equation (6.13) relates Γ_0 with lift coefficient and hence incidence; downwash angle $\epsilon = W(\text{total})/U$, so that the required $d\epsilon/d\alpha$ is given by

$$d\epsilon/d\alpha = \frac{2a}{\pi A} \sum_{\phi\,=5°}^{85°} \frac{Wb}{\Gamma_0} \quad (2)$$

```
10      Lcs=5.7
20      A=6
30      PRINT "PLEASE INPUT THE DISTANCE BEHIND THE WING (AS A FRACTION OR MULTIPL
E"
40      PRINT "OF THE SPAN) AT WHICH THE DOWNWASH DERIVATIVE IS REQUIRED"
50      INPUT X
60      PRINT
70      PRINT "DE/DA AT ";X;" SPANS BEHIND THE WING IS:"
80      PRINT "  Vertical dist in spans              DE/DA"
90      FOR Z=-.5 TO 1 STEP .25
100       W=0
110       FOR I=1 TO 9
120        Fi=(I*10-5)*PI/180
130        Y=.5*COS(Fi)
140        Pn=SQR(Z*Z+Y*Y)
150        Pb=SQR(Pn*Pn+X*X)
160        Pm=SQR(X*X+Z*Z)
170        Wab=1/Pn*(1+X/Pb)*Y/Pn
180        Wbc=1/Pm*(2*Y/Pb)*X/Pm
190        Wcd=Wab
200        W=W+(Wab+Wbc+Wcd)*COS(Fi)*10*PI/180
210       NEXT I
220       Depsda=Lcs*W/(2*PI*PI*A)
230       PRINT USING "10X,D.DD,25X,D.DDD";Z,Depsda
240      NEXT Z
250      PRINT "PRESS RETURN FOR ANOTHER CALCULATION. TO STOP, TYPE <END>"
260      INPUT A$
270      PRINT
280      IF A$="END" THEN 300
290      GOTO 30
300      PRINT "              END OF PROGRAMME"
310      END


RUN
PLEASE INPUT THE DISTANCE BEHIND THE WING (AS A FRACTION OR MULTIPLE
OF THE SPAN) AT WHICH THE DOWNWASH DERIVATIVE IS REQUIRED

DE/DA AT  .25  SPANS BEHIND THE WING IS:
  Vertical dist in spans              DE/DA
         -.50                         .164
         -.25                         .385
        0.00                          .810
         .25                          .385
         .50                          .164
         .75                          .082
        1.00                          .047
PRESS RETURN FOR ANOTHER CALCULATION. TO STOP, TYPE <END>
```

```
PLEASE INPUT THE DISTANCE BEHIND THE WING (AS A FRACTION OR MULTIPLE
OF THE SPAN) AT WHICH THE DOWNWASH DERIVATIVE IS REQUIRED

DE/DA AT  1.5  SPANS BEHIND THE WING IS:
   Vertical dist in spans             DE/DA
            -.50                        .194
            -.25                        .342
           0.00                         .613
            .25                         .342
            .50                         .184
            .75                         .106
           1.00                         .067
PRESS RETURN FOR ANOTHER CALCULATION. TO STOP, TYPE <END>

PLEASE INPUT THE DISTANCE BEHIND THE WING (AS A FRACTION OR MULTIPLE
OF THE SPAN) AT WHICH THE DOWNWASH DERIVATIVE IS REQUIRED

DE/DA AT  3  SPANS BEHIND THE WING IS:
   Vertical dist in spans             DE/DA
            -.50                        .179
            -.25                        .336
           0.00                         .607
            .25                         .336
            .50                         .179
            .75                         .103
           1.00                         .065
PRESS RETURN FOR ANOTHER CALCULATION. TO STOP, TYPE <END>
            END OF PROGRAMME
```

Program notes

(1) Line 30 requests the operator to specify the distance behind the wing at which the downwash derivative is to be calculated. The loop from lines 90 to 240 varies the vertical position of point P from half a span below, to one span above, the wing plane.

(2) The loop from 110 to 210 calculates downwash W at point P from each of the nine elementary horseshoe vortices and accumulates these values at line 200. The distances PN, PB and PM are found in lines 140 to 160 and downwashes from AB, BC and CD are calculated at 170 to 190. The angle ϕ (Fi) ranges from 5° to (5°) 85°. dϵ/dα is found at line 220 using Equation (2).

(3) One RUN with calculations at distances of 0.25, 1.5 and 3 spans behind the wing is shown. dϵ/dα is always greatest in the plane of the wing at each of these specified distances but at over half a span above the wing plane, its value appears to be largest (of the three stations considered) at 1.5 spans.

6.3   MONOPLEQN: calculation of the lift and induced drag coefficients, and the spanwise loading distribution of a specified wing, using the monoplane equation

This program inputs wing dimensions, incidence and the properties of the aerofoil section (assumed to be constant across the span) and uses the monoplane Equation (6.23) to find the first four coefficients of the Fourier series (6.18) which defines the spanwise loading distribution. (The program finds four terms only in order not to overload computing capabilities; if your computer is able to invert $N \times N$ matrices, then you may use the program (with slight modification) to find N coefficients.)

Four values of ϕ at 22.5, 45, 67.5 and 90° are substituted into Equation (6.23), producing 4 values, B_n, from the left-hand side and a 4×4 array of coefficients, M_a, of the Fourier coefficients A_1, A_3, A_5 and A_7 from the right-hand side. The program then inverts matrix, M_a, multiplies it by B_n, and hence determines the Fourier coefficients. Wing properties are then found, spanwise loading is shown and induced drag is compared with that of an elliptically loaded wing at the same lift coefficient.

```
10      OPTION BASE 1
20      DIM An(4),Ma(4,4),Main(4,4),Bn(4),U(4,8),V(4)
30      REM                 DATA INPUT
40      PRINT "Please input all angles in degrees"
50      PRINT "PLEASE INPUT WING SPAN, ROOT CHORD AND TIP CHORD ";
60      INPUT B,Cr,Ct
70      PRINT B,Cr,Ct
80      S=(Cr+Ct)*B/2
90      Ar=B*B/S
100     PRINT "PLEASE INPUT TIP TWIST RELATIVE TO ROOT (Nose up positive) ";
110     INPUT Tw
120     PRINT Tw
130     PRINT "PLEASE INPUT THE AEROFOIL SECTION LIFT CURVE SLOPE(per rad) ";
140     INPUT A
150     PRINT A
160     PRINT "PLEASE INPUT THE AEROFOIL SECTION ZERO LIFT ANGLE ";
170     INPUT A10
180     PRINT A10
190     PRINT "PLEASE INPUT THE ROOT SECTION INCIDENCE ";
200     INPUT Alr
210     PRINT Alr
220     REM         CALCULATES THE COEFFICIENTS OF THE FOURIER EXPANSIONS
230     REM         AT PHI=22.5,45,67.5 AND 90 DEGREES, AND PRINTS THEM
240     PRINT
250     PRINT " ARRAY OF EQUATION COEFFICIENTS IS:-"
260     E=22.5
270     FOR I=1 TO 4
280       Fi=I*E*PI/180
290       Al=(Alr+Tw*COS(Fi)-A10)*PI/180
300       Ch=Cr-(Cr-Ct)*COS(Fi)
310       Bn(I)=Ch*A*Al/(4*B)*SIN(Fi)
320       FOR J=1 TO 4
330         Ma(I,J)=SIN((2*J-1)*Fi)*(SIN(Fi)+(2*J-1)*Ch*A/(4*B))
340         PRINT USING "DD.DDDD,XX,#";Ma(I,J)
350       NEXT J
360       PRINT
370     NEXT I
380     REM             FINDS Main, THE INVERSE MATRIX OF Ma, AND PRINTS IT
390     D2=1
400     FOR I=1 TO 4
410       FOR J=1 TO 4
420         U(I,J)=Ma(I,J)
430         IF I=J THEN 460
440         U(I,J+4)=0
450         GOTO 470
460         U(I,J+4)=1
470       NEXT J
480       V(I)=I
490     NEXT I
500     FOR I=1 TO 4
510       M=0
520       FOR J=I TO 4
530         IF M>ABS(U(I,J)) THEN 560
540         M=ABS(U(I,J))
550         R=J
```

```
560      NEXT J
570      IF I=4 THEN 680
580      IF R=I THEN 680
590      D2=D2*(-1)
600      FOR J=1 TO 8
610       T=U(I,J)
620       U(I,J)=U(R,J)
630       U(R,J)=T
640      NEXT J
650      T=V(R)
660      V(R)=V(I)
670      C(I)=T
680      D=U(I,I)
690      D2=D2*D
700      FOR J=I TO 8
710       U(I,J)=U(I,J)/D
720      NEXT J
730      FOR Ii=1 TO 4
740       IF Ii=I THEN 790
750       D=U(Ii,I)
760       FOR J=I TO 8
770        U(Ii,J)=U(Ii,J)-D*U(I,J)
780       NEXT J
790      NEXT Ii
800     NEXT I
810     PRINT
820     PRINT "INVERSE MATRIX IS:"
830     FOR I=1 TO 4
840      FOR J=1 TO 4
850       Main(I,J)=U(I,J+4)
860       PRINT USING "DD.DDDD,XX,#";Main(I,J)
870      NEXT J
880      PRINT
890     NEXT I
900     REM         MULTIPLY THE INVERSE MATRIX BY THE COLUMN VECTOR Bn
910     REM                AND PRINT THE RESULT
920     PRINT
930     PRINT "FOURIER COEFFICIENTS ARE:-"
940     FOR I=1 TO 4
950      An(I)=0
960      FOR J=1 TO 4
970       An(I)=An(I)+Main(I,J)*Bn(J)
980      NEXT J
990      PRINT "A";2*I-1;" = ";An(I)
1000    NEXT I
1010    PRINT "                              Press RETURN when ready."
1020    INPUT A$
1030    REM                 PRINTS OUT RESULTS FOR THE WING
1040    PRINT "ASPECT RATIO = ",Ar
1050    PRINT "TAPER RATIO = ",Ct/Cr
1060    PRINT "ROOT INCIDENCE = ",Alr
1070    PRINT "WASHOUT = ",-Tw
1080    PRINT
1090    Cl=PI*Ar*An(1)
1100    PRINT USING "5A,D.DDDD";"Cl = ",Cl
1110    Cdi=0
1120    FOR I=1 TO 4
1130     Cdi=Cdi+(2*I-1)*An(I)*An(I)
1140    NEXT I
1150    Cdi=Cdi*PI*Ar
1160    PRINT USING "6A,D.DDDDD";"Cdi = ",Cdi
1170    PRINT USING "24A,D.DDDDD";"Elliptic loading Cdi = ",Cl*Cl/(PI*Ar)
1180    REM                 OUTPUTS LOCAL Cl ACROSS THE SPAN
1190    PRINT
1200    PRINT "THE SPANWISE Cl DISTRIBUTION IS:-"
1210    PRINT "  Phi          Local Cl      COS(Phi)       LOCAL CL/WING CL"
1220    FOR Phi=0 TO 90 STEP 10
1230     Fi=Phi*PI/180
1240     Lc=0
1250     FOR I=1 TO 4
1260      Lc=Lc+An(I)*SIN((2*I-1)*Fi)
1270     NEXT I
1280                 IF Ct=0 AND Phi=0 THEN 1310
1290     Lc=4*B*Lc/(Cr-(Cr-Ct)*COS(Fi))
1300     GOTO 1320
1310     Lc=99.9999
1320     PRINT USING "2X,DD,10X,DDD.DDDD,10X,D.DD,10X,DDD.DDDD";Phi,Lc,COS(Fi),Lc
/Cl
1330    NEXT Phi
1340    END
```

```
RUN
Please input all angles in degrees
PLEASE INPUT WING SPAN, ROOT CHORD AND TIP CHORD  4.5       .6        .6
PLEASE INPUT TIP TWIST RELATIVE TO ROOT (Nose up positive)  0
PLEASE INPUT THE AEROFOIL SECTION LIFT CURVE SLOPE(per rad)  6.284
PLEASE INPUT THE AEROFOIL SECTION ZERO LIFT ANGLE -1
PLEASE INPUT THE ROOT SECTION INCIDENCE  5

   ARRAY OF EQUATION COEFFICIENTS IS:-
    .2266    .9341   1.3212    .7076
    .6481    .9443  -1.2406  -1.5368
   1.0471   -.5940   -.7544   2.2082
   1.2095  -1.6284   2.0473  -2.4663

   INVERSE MATRIX IS:
    .2596    .3762    .4182    .2145
    .4465    .2933   -.1057   -.1493
    .3367   -.1848   -.0998    .1224
    .1120   -.1626    .1920   -.1001

FOURIER COEFFICIENTS ARE:-
A 1  =  .0211950597914
A 3  =  .00287983408625
A 5  =  .00062104928926
A 7  =  .000114096892263
                                        Press RETURN when ready.
ASPECT RATIO =          7.5
TAPER RATIO =           1
ROOT INCIDENCE =        5
WASHOUT =   0

Cl =  .4994
Cdi =  .01122
Elliptic loading Cdi =    .01058

THE SPANWISE Cl DISTRIBUTION IS:-
    Phi        Local Cl       COS(Phi)        LOCAL CL/WING CL
     0          0.0000         1.00             0.0000
    10           .1711          .98              .3426
    20           .3128          .94              .6264
    30           .4119          .87              .8248
    40           .4738          .77              .9487
    50           .5122          .64             1.0256
    60           .5375          .50             1.0763
    70           .5537          .34             1.1087
    80           .5622          .17             1.1257
    90           .5647         0.00             1.1307


RUN
Please input all angles in degrees
PLEASE INPUT WING SPAN, ROOT CHORD AND TIP CHORD  4.5       .7        .3
PLEASE INPUT TIP TWIST RELATIVE TO ROOT (Nose up positive)  0
PLEASE INPUT THE AEROFOIL SECTION LIFT CURVE SLOPE(per rad)  6.284
PLEASE INPUT THE AEROFOIL SECTION ZERO LIFT ANGLE -1
PLEASE INPUT THE ROOT SECTION INCIDENCE  5

   ARRAY OF EQUATION COEFFICIENTS IS:-
    .1906    .6733    .8865    .4555
    .6030    .8089  -1.0149  -1.2209
   1.0300   -.5728   -.7189   2.0884
   1.2444  -1.7331   2.2219  -2.7106

   INVERSE MATRIX IS:
    .3468    .4257    .4240    .1933
    .6195    .3225   -.1314   -.1424
    .4959   -.2328   -.0947    .1152
    .1696   -.2016    .2011   -.0947

FOURIER COEFFICIENTS ARE:-
A 1  =  .0189727472143
A 3  =  .00027040943573
A 5  =  .00098168402184
A 7  = -9.93781443374E-5
                                        Press RETURN when ready.
ASPECT RATIO =          9
TAPER RATIO =           .428571428571
ROOT INCIDENCE =        5
WASHOUT =   0
```

```
Cl =  .5364
Cdi =  .01032
Elliptic loading Cdi =    .01018

THE SPANWISE Cl DISTRIBUTION IS:-
   Phi         Local Cl        COS(Phi)      LOCAL CL/WING CL
    0          0.0000           1.00            0.0000
   10           .2404            .98             .4482
   20           .4235            .94             .7895
   30           .5242            .87             .9772
   40           .5576            .77            1.0394
   50           .5594            .64            1.0428
   60           .5578            .50            1.0398
   70           .5576            .34            1.0395
   80           .5457            .17            1.0172
   90           .5087           0.00             .9483
```

Program notes

(1) OPTION BASE 1 in line 10 defines the default lower bound of arrays to be 1 (and not 0).

(2) Line 20 dimensions the arrays to be used in the program. These are: An – the four Fourier coefficients sought; Ma – the 4 × 4 array of coefficients of A1 to A7 obtained from the right-hand side of Equation (6.23) at the four values of ϕ specified above; Main – the inverse of Ma; Bn – the array of four left-hand side values from Equation (6.23); U and V – arrays used in the matrix inversion procedure. Lines 30 to 210 take input.

(3) Lines 220 to 370 calculate the LHS values and the RHS coefficients of Equation (6.23) at the four values of ϕ. These form matrices, Bn and Ma. Ma is printed by line 340 which displays each element in the form DD.DDDD followed by two spaces; the # symbol suppresses the normal CR/LF after each numerical output.

(4) Lines 380 to 800 find Main, the inverse of Ma, using a Gaussian method with partial pivoting; if a matrix inversion statement (for example: Main = INV(Ma)) is available, then it may replace 380 to 800. The inverse is printed at 810 to 890. Lines 900 to 1000 multiply the inverse matrix Main by Bn to obtain the required Fourier coefficients in the array; these are printed.

(5) Line 1010 stops the flow of output data until the operator is ready.

(6) Lines 1030 to 1170 print further output of interest and lines 1180 to 1330 give the spanwise loading distribution.

(7) Two RUNs are shown, the first for a rectangular wing and the second for a tapered wing. Note the position of maximum local loading on each wing; at high incidence, this is where stalling will commence. The results also show the higher induced drag coefficients of non-elliptically loaded wings.

**Example 6.4   VORLAT: application of the vortex lattice method
to the calculation of lifting properties of a swept wing**

Lifting line theory, as used in Examples 6.1 to 6.3, is not
satisfactory for the prediction of flows around swept or delta
wings. This program calculates the lift curve slope of such a wing
using the vortex lattice equations of Section 6.4. The wing is of
unit span and the program operator may interactively specify the
root and tip chord lengths and the leading edge sweepback angle.
The wing surface is divided into 12 panels numbered as shown in
Figure 6.13.

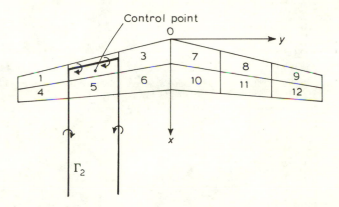

Figure 6.13   2 × 6 vortex lattice showing horseshoe vortex and
control point of panel 2

As described in Section 6.4, a bound vortex is carried by the
quarter chord line of each panel and from the end points of each of
these bound vortices, two trailing vortices run off in the
downstream direction (shown for panel 2). The control points are
centrally sited spanwise in each panel at the three quarter chord
points. Wing symmetry requires that the vortex strengths of
symmetrically positioned pairs of panels should be equal, e.g. $\Gamma 2$
$= \Gamma 8$. There are therefore six unknown vortex strengths Γ_i to be
found.

This program is a relatively long one, although 43 statements are
required for the matrix inversion and many lines are used to
output intermediate results of interests; the main stages in the
program are described in the program notes.

```
10      OPTION BASE 1
20      PRINT CHR$(12)
30      DEG
40      PRINT "Please input ROOT CHORD and TIP CHORD as fractions of the span."
50      INPUT Cr,Ct
60      PRINT Cr,Ct
70      PRINT "Please input the leading edge SWEEPBACK ANGLE in degrees."
80      INPUT L
90      PRINT L
100     M=2
110     N=6
120     Tot=M*N
130     N1=Tot/2
140     DIM Xl(12),Yl(12),Xr(12),Yr(12),Xc(12),Yc(12)
150     FOR I=1 TO M
160       Xtip(I)=.5*TAN(L)+Ct/M*(I-.75)
170       Ytip(I)=-.5
180       Xroot(I)=Cr/M*(I-.75)
190       Yroot(I)=0
200       FOR J=1 TO N/2
210         K=(I-1)*N/2+J
220         K1=Tot/2+N/2*I+1-J
230         Xl(K)=Xtip(I)-(Xtip(I)-Xroot(I))/(N/2)*(J-1)
240         Yl(K)=Ytip(I)+(Yroot(I)-Ytip(I))/(N/2)*(J-1)
250         Xr(K)=Xl(K)-(Xtip(I)-Xroot(I))/(N/2)
260         Yr(K)=Yl(K)+(Yroot(I)-Ytip(I))/(N/2)
270         Xr(K1)=Xl(K)
280         Yr(K1)=-Yl(K)
290         Xl(K1)=Xr(K)
300         Yl(K1)=-Yr(K)
310       NEXT J
320     NEXT I
330     PRINT "PANEL NUMBERS and COORDINATES of the bound vortex end points."
340     IMAGE DD,5X,2(SDDD.DDD),5X,2(SDDD.DDD)
350     FOR K=1 TO Tot
360       PRINT USING 340;K,Xl(K),Yl(K),Xr(K),Yr(K)
370     NEXT K
380     GOSUB 1710
390     FOR I=1 TO M
400       Xtip(I)=Xtip(I)+Ct/(2*M)
410       Xroot(I)=Xroot(I)+Cr/(2*M)
420       FOR J=1 TO N/2
430         K=(I-1)*N/2+J
440         K1=Tot/2+I*N/2+1-J
450         Xc(K)=Xtip(I)-(Xtip(I)-Xroot(I))/(N/2)*(J-.5)
460         Yc(K)=(Yl(K)+Yr(K))/2
470         Xc(K1)=Xc(K)
480         Yc(K1)=-Yc(K)
490       NEXT J
500     NEXT I
510     PRINT "        CONTROL POINT COORDINATES"
520     IMAGE DD,5X,2(SDDD.DDD)
530     FOR K=1 TO Tot
540       PRINT USING 520;K,Xc(K),Yc(K)
550     NEXT K
560     GOSUB 1710
570     PRINT "CALCULATIONS, FROM THIS POINT ON, ARE FOR THE LEFT WING ONLY."
580     PRINT "Values for the right wing may be obtained using the wing symmetry."
590     GOSUB 1710
600     PRINT "The matrix of computed velocities induced at each control point"
610     PRINT "on the left wing by the horseshoe vortices covering the whole"
620     PRINT "wing is proportional to:"
630     PRINT
640     DIM Ind(6,6)
650     FOR K=1 TO Tot/2
660       FOR Kk=1 TO Tot/2
670         Ind(K,Kk)=0
680       NEXT Kk
690     NEXT K
700     FOR K=1 TO Tot/2
710       FOR Kk=1 TO Tot
720         D1=SQR((Xl(Kk)-Xc(K))^2+(Yl(Kk)-Yc(K))^2)
730         D2=SQR((Xr(Kk)-Xc(K))^2+(Yr(Kk)-Yc(K))^2)
740         D3=(Xr(Kk)-Xc(K))*(Yl(Kk)-Yc(K))-(Xl(Kk)-Xc(K))*(Yr(Kk)-Yc(K))
750         D4=Yl(Kk)-Yc(K)
760         D5=Yr(Kk)-Yc(K)
770         Vbc=((Xr(Kk)-Xl(Kk))*(Xl(Kk)-Xc(K))+(Yr(Kk)-Yl(Kk))*(Yl(Kk)-Yc(K)))/D1
780         Vbc=Vbc-((Xr(Kk)-Xl(Kk))*(Xr(Kk)-Xc(K))+(Yr(Kk)-Yl(Kk))*(Yr(Kk)-Yc(K))
        )/D2
```

```
790          Vbc=Vbc/D3
800          Vab=1-(Xl(Kk)-Xc(K))/D1
810          Vab=Vab/D4
820          Vcd=1-(Xr(Kk)-Xc(K))/D2
830          Vcd=-Vcd/D5
840          W=Vab+Vbc+Vcd
850          IF Kk>Tot/2 THEN 880
860          Ind(K,Kk)=W
870          GOTO 910
880          J=INT((Kk-Tot/2-.5)/(N/2))+1
890          Kkk=(2*J-1)*(N/2)+1-(Kk-Tot/2)
900          Ind(K,Kkk)=Ind(K,Kkk)+W
910        NEXT Kk
920        FOR Kk=1 TO N1
930          PRINT USING "DDDDD.DDDDD,#";Ind(K,Kk)
940        NEXT Kk
950        PRINT
960      NEXT K
970      DIM A(6,12),C(6)
980      D2=1
990      FOR I=1 TO N1
1000       FOR J=1 TO N1
1010         A(I,J)=Ind(I,J)
1020         IF I=J THEN 1050
1030         A(I,J+N1)=0
1040         GOTO 1060
1050         A(I,J+N1)=1
1060       NEXT J
1070       C(I)=I
1080     NEXT I
1090     FOR I=1 TO N1
1100       P=0
1110       FOR J=I TO N1
1120         IF P>ABS(A(I,J)) THEN 1150
1130         P=ABS(A(I,J))
1140         R=J
1150       NEXT J
1160       IF I=N1 THEN 1270
1170       IF R=I1 THEN 1850
1180       D2=-D2
1190       FOR J=1 TO 2*N1
1200         T=A(I,J)
1210         A(I,J)=A(R,J)
1220         A(R,J)=T
1230       NEXT J
1240       T=C(R)
1250       C(R)=C(I)
1260       C(I)=T
1270       D=A(I,I)
1280       D2=D2*D
1290       FOR J=I TO 2*N1
1300         A(I,J)=A(I,J)/D
1310       NEXT J
1320       FOR Ii=1 TO N1
1330         IF Ii=I THEN 1380
1340         D=A(Ii,I)
1350         FOR J=I TO 2*N1
1360           A(Ii,J)=A(Ii,J)-D*A(I,J)
1370         NEXT J
1380       NEXT Ii
1390     NEXT I
1400     GOSUB 1710
1410     PRINT "The inverse matrix is:"
1420     FOR I=1 TO N1
1430       FOR J=1 TO N1
1440         A(I,J)=A(I,J+N1)
1450         PRINT USING "DDDDD.DDDDD,#";A(I,J)
1460       NEXT J
1470       PRINT
1480     NEXT I
1490     GOSUB 1710
1500     Gg=0
1510     PRINT "VORTEX STRENGTHS:"
1520     FOR I=1 TO N1
1530       G=0
1540       FOR J=1 TO N1
1550         G=G+A(I,J)
1560       NEXT J
1570       PRINT USING "2A,D,19A,D.DDDDD";"G(";I;")/(4.PI.b.U.alpha) ";-G
1580       Gg=Gg-G
```

```
1590    NEXT I
1600    GOSUB 1710
1610    Lcs=32*PI*Gg/((Cr+Ct)*N)
1620    IMAGE 36A,DD.DDD
1630    PRINT USING 1620;"WING LIFT CURVE SLOPE",Lcs
1640    PRINT USING 1620;"WING AREA",(Cr+Ct)/2
1650    PRINT USING 1620;"ASPECT RATIO",2/(Cr+Ct)
1660    PRINT USING 1620;"TAPER RATIO",Ct/Cr
1670    PRINT USING 1620;"LEADING EDGE SWEEPBACK ANGLE";L
1680    PRINT USING 1620;"TRAILING EDGE SWEEPBACK ANGLE";ATN((.5*TAN(L)+Ct-Cr)/.5)
1690    PRINT USING 1620;"QUARTER CHORD LINE SWEEPBACK ANGLE";ATN((.5*TAN(L)+(Ct-C
r)/4)/.5)
1700    GOTO 1750
1710    PRINT
1720    PRINT "                                                      Press RETURN"
1730    INPUT A$
1740    RETURN
1750    END
```

```
RUN
Please input ROOT CHORD and TIP CHORD as fractions of the span.
 .25         .2
Please input the leading edge SWEEPBACK ANGLE in degrees.
 33
PANEL NUMBERS and COORDINATES of the bound vortex end points.
  1      +.350   -.500        +.244   -.333
  2      +.244   -.333        +.137   -.167
  3      +.137   -.167        +.031   -0.000
  4      +.450   -.500        +.352   -.333
  5      +.352   -.333        +.254   -.167
  6      +.254   -.167        +.156   -0.000
  7      +.031  +0.000        +.137   +.167
  8      +.137   +.167        +.244   +.333
  9      +.244   +.333        +.350   +.500
 10      +.156  +0.000        +.254   +.167
 11      +.254   +.167        +.352   +.333
 12      +.352   +.333        +.450   +.500
```

Press RETURN

```
         CONTROL POINT COORDINATES
  1      +.349   -.417
  2      +.247   -.250
  3      +.145   -.083
  4      +.453   -.417
  5      +.359   -.250
  6      +.266   -.083
  7      +.145   +.083
  8      +.247   +.250
  9      +.349   +.417
 10      +.266   +.083
 11      +.359   +.250
 12      +.453   +.417
```

Press RETURN

CALCULATIONS, FROM THIS POINT ON, ARE FOR THE LEFT WING ONLY.
Values for the right wing may be obtained using the wing symmetry.

Press RETURN

The matrix of computed velocities induced at each control point
on the left wing by the horseshoe vortices covering the whole
wing is proportional to:

```
 -73.85601    14.24735     3.61977    25.60987     9.72674     3.10760
   6.91975   -70.34046    16.22003     2.57281    23.08898    10.92652
   1.44418     8.25426   -56.44429      .99041     3.11477    25.82111
 -51.20005    15.52325     3.90130   -73.12218    14.10498     3.56435
  12.62854   -50.07015    17.73590     7.30087   -69.69541    16.05860
   2.16460    14.60907   -36.11362     1.52706     8.67095   -55.91367
```

Press RETURN

```
The inverse matrix is:
   -.01129     -.00152     -.00087     -.00441     -.00333     -.00257
   -.00120     -.01234     -.00214     -.00152     -.00529     -.00508
   -.00051     -.00182     -.01418     -.00084     -.00243     -.00768
    .00749     -.00017     -.00024     -.01122     -.00140     -.00084
   -.00060      .00790     -.00029     -.00122     -.01235     -.00225
   -.00031     -.00089      .00851     -.00052     -.00189     -.01472
```

Press RETURN

```
VORTEX STRENGTHS:
G(1)/(4.PI.b.U.alpha)   .02399
G(2)/(4.PI.b.U.alpha)   .02756
G(3)/(4.PI.b.U.alpha)   .02745
G(4)/(4.PI.b.U.alpha)   .00637
G(5)/(4.PI.b.U.alpha)   .00881
G(6)/(4.PI.b.U.alpha)   .00982
```

```
                                       Press RETURN
WING LIFT CURVE SLOPE              3.873
WING AREA                           .225
ASPECT RATIO                       4.444
TAPER RATIO                         .800
LEADING EDGE SWEEPBACK ANGLE      33.000
TRAILING EDGE SWEEPBACK ANGLE     28.785
QUARTER CHORD LINE SWEEPBACK ANGLE 31.981
```

Program notes

(1) Line 10 defines the default lower bound of arrays to be 1; if your computer automatically sets the lower bound at 1; then this line can be omitted.

(2) Line 20 clears the screen; on other computers, there may be other statements which will do this.

(3) Lines 40 to 130 take in data on the unit span wing and set the number of rows and columns of wing panels to be 2 and 6 respectively.

(4) Lines 140 to 550 calculate the coordinates of the end points of the bound vortex and the control point of each panel; these are stored in arrays (X1), (Y1); (Xr), (Yr) and (Xc), (Yc) (left, right and control) and are printed with appropriate headings.

(5) Lines 640 to 960 use Equation (6.24) 72 times to calculate the contribution from each of the 12 panels to the induced velocity at each of the six control points on the left-hand wing. This information is stored in the 6×6 array, Ind, and is printed.

(6) Lines 970 to 1390 invert the matrix, Ind. If a single matrix inversion statement is available on your computer, e.g. A = INV(Ind) then it should be used and line 1440 should also be omitted. Lines 1430 to 1480 print the inverse.

(7) Lines 1500 to 1690 compute the non-dimensional vortex strengths followed by wing characteristics, which are then output.

(8) After printing each set of output values, the program goes to a subroutine at line 1710; this stops the computation to allow the operator time to study the output if he/she desires. Pressing RETURN will restart the program.

(9) With slight modification, the program will handle different arrays of panels from the 2×6 array used above. There will be a

124   Finite wing theory

limit on your computer's ability to invert the matrix, Ind, which will prevent large panel arrays from being attempted. If a different panel arrangement is required, then appropriate changes are needed to statements 100, 110, 140, 640 and 970.

Example 6.5   DELTAWING: an investigation of the lift and drag characteristics of a slender delta wing at low Mach number

Equation (6.41), and the comment following, shows that the lift/drag ratio of a high aspect ratio unswept wing rises to a typical maximum value of about 22 at an incidence of about 4° assuming a lift curve slope of 5.73. To illustrate the differences between the properties of this type of wing and a low aspect ratio delta, this program calculates lift and drag coefficients and lift/drag ratio of a delta wing of aspect ratio 1 using Equations (6.35) and (6.39) over a range of incidence angles from 0 to 24. Results of interest are printed at 2° intervals.

```
10      PRINT
20      PRINT "INC          LIFT COEFFT                    DRAG COEFFT             LIFT
/DRAG RATIO"
30      PRINT "        Pot'l   Vortex    Total      Pot'l   Vortex    Total"
40      Cd0=.008
50      Kp=1.30
60      Kv=PI
70      Ld0=0
80      A10=0
90      FOR A1=0 TO 24 STEP .25
100     A=A1*PI/180
110     Clp=Kp*SIN(A)*COS(A)*COS(A)
120     Clv=Kv*SIN(A)*SIN(A)*COS(A)
130     Cl=Clp+Clv
140     Cdp=Clp*TAN(A)
150     Cdv=Clv*TAN(A)
160     Cdi=Cdp+Cdv
170     Cd=Cd0+Cdi
180     Ld=Cl/Cd
190     IF Ld<Ld0 THEN 220
200     Ld0=Ld
210     A10=A1
220     IF INT(A1/2)<>A1/2 THEN 240
230     PRINT USING "DD,5X,3(D.DDDD,2X),4X,3(D.DDDD,2X),8X,D.DDDD";A1,Clp,Clv,Cl
,Cdp,Cdv,Cd,Ld
240     NEXT A1
250     PRINT
260     PRINT "Maximum lift/drag ratio is ";Ld0;" at ";A10;" degrees incidence."
270     END

RUN
```

INC	LIFT COEFFT			DRAG COEFFT			LIFT/DRAG RATIO
	Pot'l	Vortex	Total	Pot'l	Vortex	Total	
0	0.0000	0.0000	0.0000	0.0000	0.0000	.0080	0.0000
2	.0453	.0038	.0491	.0016	.0001	.0097	5.0575
4	.0902	.0152	.1055	.0063	.0011	.0154	6.8605
6	.1344	.0341	.1685	.0141	.0036	.0257	6.5543
8	.1774	.0603	.2377	.0249	.0085	.0414	5.7405
10	.2189	.0933	.3122	.0386	.0164	.0631	4.9517
12	.2586	.1328	.3914	.0550	.0282	.0912	4.2920
14	.2961	.1784	.4745	.0738	.0445	.1263	3.7567
16	.3311	.2294	.5605	.0949	.0658	.1687	3.3221
18	.3634	.2853	.6487	.1181	.0927	.2188	2.9651
20	.3926	.3453	.7379	.1429	.1257	.2766	2.6680
22	.4186	.4088	.8274	.1691	.1651	.3423	2.4172
24	.4413	.4748	.9161	.1965	.2114	.4159	2.2028

Maximum lift/drag ratio is 6.89607310179 at 4.5 degrees incidence.

Program notes

(1) Lines 40 to 60 specify a value for the viscous drag coefficient CD0 as 0.008, and the values of Kp and Kv appropriate to an AR of 1 are 1.3 and 0.0 respectively.

(2) Lines 70 and 80 set the starting values of L/D(max) and the incidence at which it occurs (LD0 and A10) at zero.

(3) Lines 90 to 180 calculate C1, Cd and L/D at incidences from 0 to 24° in quarter degree steps. At each incidence, L/D is compared with LD0 and if it is greater it replaces the current value of LD0 and A10 is updated (lines 190 to 210).

(4) Line 220 prevents output from being printed unless the incidence is an even integer.

(5) Note that the vortex lift and drag forces contribute more and more to the total lift and drag as incidence increases, becoming, in this example, equal to potential forces at about 22°. At low Mach numbers, it can be seen that the best lift/drag ratio, a measure of wing efficiency in cruise, is only 7 – a poor value compared with the high aspect ratio unswept wing.

PROBLEMS

(6.1) Extend the program BIRDDRAG (Example 6.1) so that the number of birds, their dimensions, masses and spacings may be entered interactively from the keyboard and the program then prints out the induced velocities at all the bird positions as well as the induced drag force acting on each bird. Investigate the proposition that the middle bird always comes off best. How does the number of birds affect drag reduction?

(6.2) The effect of the presence of the ground on the flow around a wing may be modelled by adding to the wing's vortex system, the image vortex system in the ground plane. Write a program which will input wing dimensions, speed and lift force and, assuming constant spanwise loading, calculate the sealevel downwash at the wing centre line (a) out of ground effect and (b) in ground effect at a specified altitude h. Assuming these downwash values are appropriate across the whole span of the wing, compare the induced drags in and out of ground effect.

(6.3) Write a program to input delta wing dimensions and incidence and then integrate Equation (6.31) numerically over the wing surface (taking care to avoid the singularities along the leading edge) to determine the lift force. Confirm that the result agrees with Equations (6.32) and (6.33).

(**6.4**) An elliptically loaded wing is twisted so that the local geometric incidence is described by

$$\alpha = \alpha_0 + \tau(1 - \sin \phi)$$

where α_0 is the wing root incidence and τ is the (small) relative twist between tips and root. Write a program which, for an input twist angle (positive or negative), will output chord lengths from ϕ = 0 to 90°, in steps of 5°. The program will be based on a solution for c of Equation (6.16) and should use suitable values for wing span, speed, aerofoil section lift curve slope and root incidence. Check results at $\tau = 0$ with Equation (6.17).

(**6.5**) Using the data and panel dimensions of the wing of Example Program 6.4, write a program to calculate the velocities induced by the horseshoe vortices of panel 1 and panel 9 at the control point of panel 5. Use the value of Γ_1 calculated in the example run, i.e. $G(1)/4\pi bU = 0.02399$.

(**6.6**) Assuming that the variation of K_p and K_v with aspect ratio shown in Figure 6.8 may be approximated by linear equations, find suitable relations between K_p and K_v and aspect ratio, and write a program, similar to Example 6.5, which will investigate the effect of aspect ratio on the maximum lift/drag ratio of a delta wing.

Chapter 7

Supersonic flow

ESSENTIAL THEORY

7.1 Introduction

The influence of Mach number, M, on compressible flows has already been noted in Sections 2.5 and 5.1 and this parameter is of dominating importance in supersonic flow. Along a streamline in steady, adiabatic supersonic flow, stagnation temperature, as defined by Equation (2.19), remains constant but stagnation pressure, as defined by Equation (2.18), is constant only in isentropic flow (in practice, this means inviscid, shock free flow).

Mach cone

Weak pressure disturbances emitted by a point moving at supersonic Mach number M will be confined to a conical volume (Mach cone) with semi-vertex angle, called the Mach angle, given by

$$\mu = \sin^{-1}(1/M) \tag{7.1}$$

7.2 One-dimensional flow

Isentropic flow between nearly parallel streamlines may be analysed as if it were one dimensional. Along such a 'duct', the mass continuity Equation (2.12), the differential form of the energy Equation (2.15) and Equation (2.3) may be combined to give

$$\frac{(M^2 - 1)}{V} dV = \frac{1}{A} dA \tag{7.2}$$

indicating that, under supersonic conditions, an increase in cross sectional area will be associated with an increase in velocity and vice versa, whereas at subsonic speeds, an area increase leads to a velocity decrease. Sonic conditions (M = 1) only occur at dA = 0, i.e. at a local minimum area, or throat. If conditions at a throat are denoted by asterisked symbols, then it may be shown that general conditions along the duct can be expressed in terms of the area ratio A/A^*. In particular

$$\left(\frac{A^*}{A}\right)^2 = M^2 \left\{\frac{2}{\gamma + 1}\left(1 + \frac{(\gamma - 1)\, M^2}{2}\right)\right\}^{-(\gamma + 1)/(\gamma - 1)} \quad (7.3)$$

and

$$\left(\frac{A}{A_*}\right)^2 = \frac{\dfrac{(\gamma - 1)}{2}\left(\dfrac{2}{\gamma + 1}\right)^{(\gamma + 1)/(\gamma - 1)}}{\left[1 - \left(\dfrac{p}{p_{ST}}\right)^{(\gamma - 1)/\gamma}\right]\left(\dfrac{p}{p_{ST}}\right)^{2/\gamma}} \quad (7.4)$$

also

$$\left(\frac{\dot{m}}{A}\right)^2 = \frac{2\gamma}{\gamma - 1}\, p_{ST}\rho_{ST}\left(\frac{p}{p_{ST}}\right)^{2/\gamma}\left[1 - \left(\frac{p}{p_{ST}}\right)^{(\gamma - 1)/\gamma}\right] \quad (7.5)$$

Equation (7.5) is known as the St Venant equation. Relations between throat and stagnation conditions are

$$\frac{p^*}{p_{ST}} = \left(\frac{2}{\gamma + 1}\right)^{\gamma/(\gamma - 1)} \qquad = 0.528 \text{ for air} \quad (7.6)$$

$$\frac{T^*}{T_{ST}} = \frac{2}{\gamma + 1} \qquad = 0.833 \text{ for air} \quad (7.7)$$

$$\frac{\dot{m}}{a^*} = \gamma\left(\frac{2}{\gamma + 1}\right)^{(\gamma + 1)/(\gamma - 1)} p_{ST}\rho_{ST} = 0.469 \text{ for air} \quad (7.8)$$

After passing through a throat, the flow either accelerates supersonically or decelerates subsonically, and the supersonic acceleration may itself terminate at a normal shock returning conditions to subsonic; the actual flow downstream of the throat depends upon the duct exit pressure.

7.3   Shock waves

A succession of compression pulses will tend to coalesce into a single, discontinuous, adiabatic but non-isentropic compression called a shock wave. A succession of rarefactions will spread out spatially and no rarefaction front can ever form. Supersonic flow decelerates through a shock wave and, if the shock is not perpendicular to the flow direction, a flow deflection occurs.

7.3.1 Shock equations

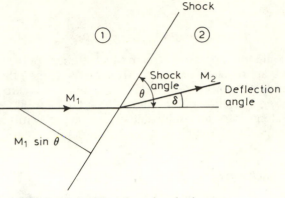

Figure 7.1 Flow through a shock wave

Application of the continuity, momentum and energy equations to conditions across a shock leads to the following results:

Flow deflection angle:

$$\delta = \tan^{-1}\left[\frac{2\cot\theta\,(M_1^2\sin^2\theta - 1)}{M_1^2\,(\gamma + \cos 2\theta) + 2}\right] \quad (7.9)$$

Pressure ratio:

$$\frac{p_2}{p_1} = \frac{2\gamma M_1^2\sin^2\theta - (\gamma - 1)}{\gamma + 1} \quad (7.10)$$

Temperature ratio:

$$\frac{T_2}{T_1} = \frac{[2\gamma M_1^2\sin^2\theta - (\gamma - 1)]\,[(\gamma - 1)\,M_1^2\sin^2\theta + 2]}{(\gamma + 1)^2\,M_1^2\sin^2\theta} \quad (7.11)$$

Density ratio:

$$\frac{\rho_2}{\rho_1} = \frac{p_2 T_1}{p_1 T_2} = \frac{(\gamma + 1)\,M_1^2\sin^2\theta}{(\gamma - 1)\,M_1^2\sin^2\theta + 2} \quad (7.12)$$

Mach number:

$$M_2^2 = \frac{(\gamma - 1)\,M_1^2\sin^2\theta + 2}{[2\gamma\,M_1^2\sin^2\theta - (\gamma - 1)]\,\sin^2(\theta - \delta)} \quad (7.13)$$

where suffixes 1 and 2 refer to conditions upstream and downstream of the shock, θ is the shock angle and δ is the flow deflection angle. Stagnation temperature remains constant but stagnation pressure decreases:

$$\frac{p_{ST_2}}{p_{ST_1}} = \left(\frac{p_1}{p_2}\right)^{1/(\gamma-1)} \left(\frac{\rho_2}{\rho_1}\right)^{\gamma/(\gamma-1)} \tag{7.14}$$

As the component of the upstream Mach number perpendicular to the shock approaches unity, i.e. $M_1 \sin \theta \to 1$, then the pressure ratio tends to unity, deflection angle tends to zero, entropy increase tends to zero and the shock is said to be weak, eventually degenerating into an isentropic Mach wave with zero flow deflection.

Normal shock wave

When $\theta = \pi/2$, the shock is normal to the flow, deflection is zero and the downstream Mach number is always subsonic. The relation between upstream and downstream velocities is then

$$v_1 v_2 = a^{*2} \qquad \text{with} \qquad v_1 > v_2 \tag{7.15}$$

where a^* is related to stagnation temperature by Equations (2.3) and (7.7).

Plane oblique shock wave

At any given upstream Mach number, M_1, there is a maximum flow deflection angle δ which increases to a value of about 46° as $M_1 \to \infty$. Flow deflections less than this maximum can be produced at two different wave angles; one of these results in a weak shock with a supersonic downstream Mach number except when the deflection is near the maximum (within one degree), and the other results in a strong shock with subsonic downstream Mach number.

Conical oblique shock wave

Although based on the same principles of continuity of mass, momentum and energy, the equations describing conditions across an axisymmetric shock wave are different from those of a plane wave. In particular, flow deflections around a conical nose occur both at the shock and downstream of it; the maximum possible flow deflection angle is greater than that of plane flow at the same upstream Mach number.

7.4   Supersonic flow over curved surfaces and at corners

7.4.1   Flow over a convex surface

Supersonic flow over a convex surface accelerates through an infinite series of infinitely small expansion waves which deflect the flow parallel to the surface.

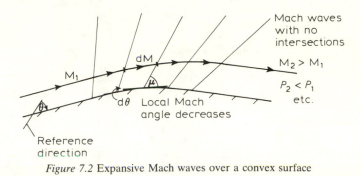

Figure 7.2 Expansive Mach waves over a convex surface

An expansive change in flow direction $d\theta$ is related to the corresponding increase in Mach number dM by

$$d\theta = \frac{(M^2 - 1)^{1/2}\, dM}{M\,(1 + (\gamma - 1)\,M^2/2)} \tag{7.16}$$

which may be integrated to

$$\theta = \nu + \text{constant} \tag{7.17}$$

where ν is a function of M:

$$\nu = \sqrt{\frac{\gamma + 1}{\gamma - 1}}\, \tan^{-1} \sqrt{\frac{(\gamma - 1)\,(M^2 - 1)}{\gamma + 1}} - \tan^{-1}\sqrt{M^2 - 1} \tag{7.18}$$

Along the expansion lines of Figure 7.2 (left running characteristics), the function $(\theta - \nu)$ is therefore constant. As M increases around the corner, pressure decreases in accordance with Equation (2.18). Theoretically, the minimum possible absolute pressure is zero, with M tending to infinity and ν tending to about 130.45°; the difference between this angle and the upstream value of ν gives the maximum possible flow deflection angle – a function of upstream Mach number. In practice, real fluid effects limit the minimum pressure to about 30% of the upstream value.

Convex corner

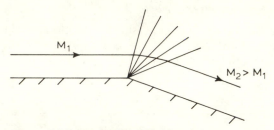

Figure 7.3 Expansive (Prandtl–Meyer) fan at a corner

At a sharp corner, all the expansion lines emanate from the corner point, producing a Prandtl–Meyer expansion fan to which Equations (7.17), (7.18) and isentropic one-dimensional flow equations apply.

7.4.2   Flow over a concave surface

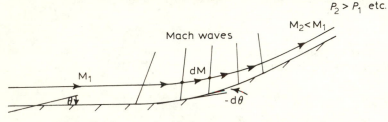

Figure 7.4 Compressive Mach waves over a concave surface

Flow over a concave surface is compressive and fluid close to the surface is decelerated through an infinite series of infinitely small compression waves where now

$$-d\theta = \frac{(M^2 - 1)^{1/2}\, dM}{M\,(1 + (\gamma - 1)\,M^2/2)} \tag{7.19}$$

which integrates to

$$\theta = -\nu + \text{constant} \tag{7.20}$$

with ν given by Equation (7.18). Along the compression lines of Figure 7.4 (right running characteristics), the function $(\theta + \nu)$ is constant close to the surface. However, away from the surface successive compression lines intersect and the infinitely small pressure increments across each wave build up into a finite, non-isentropic compression, i.e. a shock wave.

Concave corner

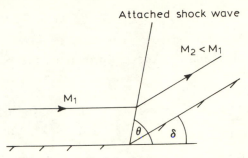

Figure 7.5 Attached shock at a concave corner

At a sharp corner, an oblique shock will emanate from the corner point provided the corner angle δ does not exceed the maximum possible flow deflection angle appropriate to M_1, as discussed in Section 7.3. If δ exceeds this maximum, the shock will detach and form ahead of the corner. This detached shock is normal to the flow close to the upstream wall of the corner producing an area of subsonic flow and high pressures in the corner region.

7.5   Supersonic aerofoil sections

The leading edge of aerofoils for supersonic flight must be sharp, or blunted only a very small amount, in order to attach the shock to the leading edge; if the leading edge is not sharp, the nose shock will be detached resulting in high wave drag. Another feature required for low pressure drag is a very low thickness/chord ratio.

7.5.1   Ackeret linear theory

For small flow deflection angles, the pressure waves generated at a sharp leading edge and over the upper and lower surfaces of a thin aerofoil may be assumed weak and isentropic, so that the pressure coefficient may be expressed in terms of the flow deflection angle δ by

$$C_p = \frac{2\delta}{\sqrt{M^2 - 1}} \qquad (7.21)$$

δ is positive if it results in a compressive change in flow direction.

From this result, lift coefficient at incidence α may be shown to be

$$C_L = \frac{4\alpha}{\sqrt{M^2 - 1}} \qquad (7.22)$$

for any camber and thickness distribution; the pressure drag coefficient is

$$C_D = \frac{4}{\sqrt{M^2 - 1}} \left[\alpha^2 + \frac{1}{2c} \int_0^c \left(\frac{dz_u}{dx}\right)^2 + \left(\frac{dz_l}{dx}\right)^2 dx \right] \qquad (7.23)$$

where dz_u/dx and dz_l/dx are the slopes of the upper and lower surfaces relative to the chord line. For an aerofoil with zero camber

$$C_D = \frac{4}{\sqrt{M^2 - 1}} (\alpha^2 + K\tau^2) \qquad (7.24)$$

where τ is the thickness/chord ratio and K is a factor dependant on aerofoil section shape, e.g. a flat plate has $K = 0$, a symmetrical double wedge has $K = 1$ (the minimum possible value for non-zero τ) and a biconvex aerofoil has $K = 4/3$. The presence of the τ^2 term shows the importance of low thickness/chord ratio at supersonic speeds; also to be noted is the decrease in both lift and drag coefficients with increasing Mach number. The two terms of Equations (7.23) and (7.24) are referred to as wave drag due to lift and wave drag due to thickness respectively. Skin friction drag coefficient at the appropriate Reynolds and Mach numbers must be added to give total drag. The centre of pressure of all symmetric aerofoils is at the mid-chord point.

7.5.2   Busemann's second order theory

A more accurate expression for the pressure coefficient on a surface inclined at an angle δ to freestream direction is

$$C_p = C_1\delta + C_2\delta^2 \qquad (7.25)$$

where

$$C_1 = \frac{2}{\sqrt{M^2 - 1}} \qquad (7.26)$$

$$C_2 = \frac{(\gamma + 1)M^4 - 4M^2 + 4}{2(M^2 - 1)^2} \qquad (7.27)$$

The first term is the same as the Ackeret linear expression; the second term is always positive and, in practice, has negligible effect on the integrated lift and drag forces acting on the complete aerofoil.

7.5.3   Shock expansion theory

For the most accurate determination of surface pressures in supersonic flow, the oblique shock Equations (7.9) to (7.14) must be used for compressive flow through shock waves, and the Prandtl–Meyer Equations (7.17), (7.18) and (2.18) for expansive flow over convex surfaces.

7.5.4   Swept infinite span aerofoils

The results quoted thus far are for unswept aerofoil sections but the equations may be applied to aerofoils of infinite span with sweepback angle Λ, provided the leading and trailing edges are supersonic, i.e. the Mach lines are inclined at a smaller angle to the freestream than the swept edges; this condition may be written:

$$M \cos \Lambda > 1 \qquad (7.28)$$

Only the flow in the plane normal to the wing leading edge influences the lift and drag and, using simple Ackeret, two-dimensional results, it may be shown that

$$C_p = \frac{2\alpha_e}{\sqrt{M_e^2 - 1}} \simeq \frac{2\alpha}{\sqrt{M^2 - \sec^2\Lambda}} \qquad (7.29)$$

$$C_L = \frac{4\alpha_e}{\sqrt{M_e^2 - 1}} \left(\frac{M_e}{M}\right)^2 \simeq \frac{4\alpha}{\sqrt{M^2 - \sec^2 \Lambda}} \qquad (7.30)$$

where α_e and M_e are respectively the effective incidence and Mach number in the plane normal to the leading edge.

$$\alpha_e = \tan^{-1} \left(\frac{\tan \alpha}{\cos \Lambda}\right) \simeq \alpha \sec \Lambda \qquad \text{for small } \alpha \qquad (7.31)$$

and

$$M_e = M(1 - \cos^2 \alpha \sin^2 \Lambda)^{1/2} \simeq M \cos \Lambda \text{ for small } \alpha \quad (7.32)$$

The corresponding wave drag is given by Equation (7.23) with M and α replaced by M_e and α_e, and upper and lower surface slopes are those in the plane perpendicular to the leading edge.

7.6   Linearized potential flow theory

A flow field which consists of small velocity perturbations u, v, w superimposed on a uniform stream U along the x-axis is described by the linearized supersonic potential equation

$$(M^2 - 1) \frac{\partial^2 \phi}{\partial x^2} - \frac{\partial^2 \phi}{\partial y^2} - \frac{\partial^2 \phi}{\partial z^2} = 0 \qquad (7.33)$$

where $M = U/a$, $u = \partial\phi/\partial x$, $v = \partial\phi/\partial y$, $w = \partial\phi/\partial z$ and ϕ is the scalar potential function.

Pressure coefficient is then:

$$C_p = -2u/U = \frac{-2}{U} \frac{\partial\phi}{\partial x} \qquad (7.34)$$

The following functions are solutions of Equation (7.33):

(1) $\phi = \dfrac{-C}{2\pi R'}$ \qquad\qquad supersonic source   (7.35)

(2) $\phi = \dfrac{C(M^2 - 1)(z - z_1)}{R'^3}$ \qquad supersonic doublet   (7.36)

(3) $\phi = \dfrac{C(z - z_1)(x - x_1)}{R'[(y - y_1)^2 + (z - z_1)^2]}$ supersonic vortex   (7.37)

where C is the strength of the element which is positioned at the singular point (x_1, y_1, z_1), and

$$R' = \{(x - x_1)^2 - (M^2 - 1)[(y - y_1)^2 + (z - z_1)^2]\}^{1/2} \quad (7.38)$$

The influence of these solutions extends only over the interior of the downstream Mach cone emanating from (x_1, y_1, z_1). These elements may be distributed and superimposed, in a manner identical to the manipulation of the incompressible elements of Chapter 3, in order to analyse specific small perturbation flows, such as a uniform stream around a slender body, wing or wing/body combination.

Two-dimensional solutions

In the $0xy$ plane, two-dimensional solutions to Equation (7.33) lead to the Ackeret and Busemann equations already introduced.

7.6.1   Pointed bodies of revolution

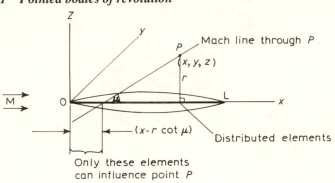

Figure 7.6 Pointed body of revolution at zero incidence

Axially symmetric flow round a slender pointed body of revolution at zero incidence may be represented by a distribution of sources along the x axis. The potential at point (x, r) where $r^2 = y^2 + z^2$ may be shown to be

$$\phi = \frac{-U}{2\pi} \int_0^{x - r \cot \mu} \frac{S'(s)\,ds}{[(x - s)^2 - (M^2 - 1)\,r^2]^{1/2}} \qquad (7.39)$$

with

$$C_p = \frac{-2}{U} \frac{\partial \phi}{\partial x} \qquad (7.40)$$

where $S(x)$ is the body cross sectional area at distance x from the pointed nose and dashes denote differentiation. Lift is, of course, zero at zero incidence; if the body is either pointed at both ends or tangential to a cylindrical extension at the aft end, then the drag is

$$\frac{D}{\tfrac{1}{2}\gamma p M^2} = \frac{1}{2\pi} \int_0^L \int_0^L \log \frac{1}{|s - x|} S''(x)\, S''(s)\, ds\, dx \qquad (7.41)$$

Further development of the theory for an axially symmetric body at incidence α gives the lift per unit axial distance as

$$\frac{d(\text{Lift})}{dx} = \tfrac{1}{2}\gamma p M^2\, 2\alpha\, S'(x) \qquad (7.42)$$

i.e. lift is positive where cross sectional area is increasing, zero with constant area and negative where S is decreasing. If the body is pointed at both ends, then the overall lift is zero but for a body with base area $S(L)$, then

$$\text{Lift} = \tfrac{1}{2}\gamma p \text{M}^2 2\alpha S(L) \tag{7.43}$$

and drag due to lift, together with base drag is

$$D = \text{Lift} \times \frac{\alpha}{2} - P_B S(L) \tag{7.44}$$

where P_B is the base pressure at incidence α. The centre of pressure is at a distance $x = L - V/S(L)$ from the nose where V is body volume and L is body length.

7.6.2   Finite aspect ratio thin symmetric wing

The wing plane of symmetry is $y = 0$. Sources, as defined by Equation (7.35), are distributed in the $z = 0$ plane over the area outlined by the wing planform and the potential at point (x, y, z) may be shown to be

$$\phi = \frac{-U}{\pi} \int\int_S \frac{\lambda \, ds \, dt}{\{(x - s)^2 - (\text{M}^2 - 1)\,[(y - t)^2 + z^2]\}^{1/2}} \tag{7.45}$$

where λ is the inclination of the wing surface to the $0x$ direction and S is the wing area in the $0xy$ plane lying inside the forward Mach cone from (x, y, z). The pressure coefficient at point $(x, y, 0)$ on the wing surface is then obtained from Equation (7.34), and lift and drag forces follow.

7.7   Supersonic finite span wings

To minimize pressure drag, the thickness/chord ratio must be kept low at supersonic speeds and hence the ability of the wing root to withstand bending moments arising from the lift will be small. This in turn requires the wing aspect ratio to be as low as possible consistent with reasonable aerodynamic efficiency.

7.7.1   Rectangular planform

The leading edge will always be supersonic and in regions R1 of Figure 7.7 the flow is two dimensional; three-dimensional effects are confined to triangular areas bound by Mach lines through the tip leading edges. If $A \cot \mu > 2$ the two tip Mach lines do not intersect ahead of the trailing edge as shown in Figure 7.7(a), but if $1 < A \cot \mu < 2$ then they will intersect simply as in Figure 7.7(b).

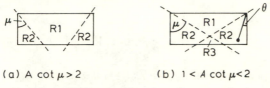

(a) $A \cot \mu > 2$ (b) $1 < A \cot \mu < 2$

Figure 7.7 Rectangular wing of aspect ratio A

Conditions within the tip Mach cones were first investigated by Busemann who found that the flow was conical, i.e. conditions were constant along lines emanating from the leading edge tips. In particular, in regions R2 of Figure 7.7, the pressure difference Δp between the upper and lower surfaces for a flat plate aerofoil is given by

$$\frac{\Delta p}{\tfrac{1}{2}\gamma p \mathrm{M}^2} = \frac{4\alpha}{\sqrt{\mathrm{M}^2 - 1}} \frac{0.2}{\pi} \sin^{-1} \left(\frac{\tan \theta}{\tan \mu}\right)^{1/2} \quad (7.46)$$

where θ is the angle between the wing tip edge and the line joining the tip leading edge to a general point in the conical flow field as shown in Figure 7.7(b). From this result, it can be shown that the mean pressure over tip triangles is half the two-dimensional value.

Integration of the pressures over a rectangular wing with $A \cot \mu > 1$ and allowing for wing thickness effects gives

$$C_{\mathrm{L}} = \frac{4\alpha}{\sqrt{\mathrm{M}^2 - 1}} \left[1 - \frac{1}{2A \sqrt{\mathrm{M}^2 - 1}} \left(1 - \frac{2C_2 A'}{C_1}\right)\right] \quad (7.47)$$

where C_1 and C_2 are Busemann coefficients defined by Equations (7.26) and (7.27), and A' is a wing thickness factor:

$$A' = \frac{\text{Aerofoil cross sectional area}}{\text{Chord squared}} \quad (7.48)$$

$$= \begin{cases} \tau/2 & \text{(double wedge)} \\ 2\tau/3 & \text{(biconvex)} \end{cases}$$

Drag coefficient is

$$C_{\mathrm{D}} = C_{\mathrm{L}}\alpha + \frac{4K\Gamma^2}{\sqrt{\mathrm{M}^2 - 1}} + C_{\mathrm{D_f}} \quad (7.49)$$

where K is defined after Equation (7.24) and C_{D_f} is friction drag coefficient. The centre of pressure position is upstream of the mid-chord point by a distance

$$x = \frac{1 + 6 \dfrac{C_2}{C_1} \; A' \, (2A \, \sqrt{M^2 - 1} - 1)}{12A \, \sqrt{M^2 - 1} - 6 + 12 \dfrac{C_2}{C_1} A'} \tag{7.50}$$

7.7.2 Swept and delta wings with supersonic leading edges

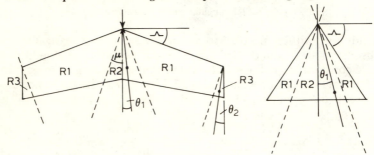

Figure 7.8 Swept and delta wings with supersonic edges

If the leading edge is supersonic, flow in areas R1 immediately downstream of the leading edge is swept aerofoil flow and in other areas the flow is conical. At small angles of incidence, the pressure loading Δp is:

In regions R1 (7.29) applies

$$\frac{\Delta p}{\frac{1}{2}\gamma p M^2} = \frac{4\alpha}{\sqrt{M^2 - \sec^2\Lambda}} \tag{7.51}$$

In regions R2:

$$\frac{\Delta p}{\frac{1}{2}\gamma p M^2} = \frac{4\alpha}{\sqrt{M^2 - \sec^2\Lambda}} \left\{ 1 - \frac{2}{\pi}\left[\frac{\tan^2\Lambda(1 - (M^2 - 1)\tan^2\theta_1)}{(M^2 - 1)(1 - \tan^2\theta_1\tan^2\Lambda)} \right] \right\} \tag{7.52}$$

In regions R3 (7.46) applies:

$$\frac{\Delta p}{\frac{1}{2}\gamma p M^2} = \frac{4\alpha}{\sqrt{M^2 - \sec^2\Lambda}} \; \frac{2}{\pi} \; \sin^{-1}\left(\frac{\tan\theta_2}{\tan\mu} \right)^{1/2} \tag{7.53}$$

θ_1 and θ_2 are defined in Figure 7.8. Lift, drag and centre of pressure position may be derived by integration of pressures over the prescribed planform geometry.

7.7.3   Swept and delta wings with subsonic leading edges

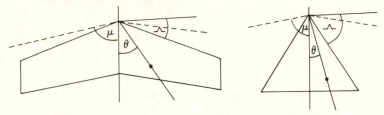

Figure 7.9 Swept and delta wings with subsonic leading edges

The subsonic delta wing flow described in Section 6.6 is maintained into the supersonic speed range for swept and delta planforms so long as the leading edges lie inside the Mach cone from the wing vertex. Pressures are found by superposition of a potential flow and a vortex flow. The potential flow pressure distribution is conical and, as in the subsonic case, C_p goes to infinity at the leading edge producing, in practice, a flow separation and leading edge vortex. The resulting delta wing lift coefficient is given by the Polhamus expression which has already appeared as Equation (6.35):

$$C_L = K_p \sin \alpha \cos^2 \alpha + K_v \sin^2 \alpha \cos \alpha \qquad (7.54)$$

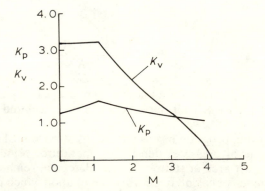

Figure 7.10 Variation of K_p and K_v with Mach number for $A = 1$

Figure 7.10 shows how K_p and K_v vary with M for a delta wing of aspect ratio 1. It will be noted that K_v goes to zero at the Mach number at which the leading edge is sonic. The centre of pressure of the potential flow component of lift is at the area centroid of a delta wing.

Reversed flow theorem

If both leading and trailing edges of a swept or delta wing are supersonic, then the overall lift and drag forces are unchanged by flow reversal.

WORKED EXAMPLES

Example 7.1   FLOWDUCT: calculation of gas properties in compressible isentropic duct flow

The flow parameters: pressure p, density ρ, temperature T, velocity V, Mach number M and duct cross sectional area A at two stations S1 and S2 in a duct or streamtube, along which the flow is compressible and isentropic, are related by the continuity Equation (2.12), Bernoulli's Equations (2.18) and (2.19), the equation of state (2.1) and the isentropic gas law (2.2). It can then be shown that the mass flow rate per unit area, $\dot{m}/A$, is given in terms of pressure, p, by the St Venant Equation (7.5). Temperature and speed are related by a slightly modified form of Equation (2.19):

$$T_{ST} = T \left(1 + \frac{(\gamma - 1)\, V^2}{2\gamma RT}\right) \qquad (1)$$

If conditions at station S1 are known, then, if just one parameter is specified at station S2, all the others can be calculated using the equations quoted above.

The following program inputs conditions at station S1 and then, given any one of pressure, density, temperature, velocity, Mach number or duct area at station S2, calculates the remainder.

The sequence of calculations will depend upon which parameter is specified at station S2 and in this kind of situation where one of several strategies may be followed depending on current conditions or information available, a *flow diagram* is a useful tool for determining the overall structure of the program; Figure 7.11 shows the flow diagram on which this program is based.

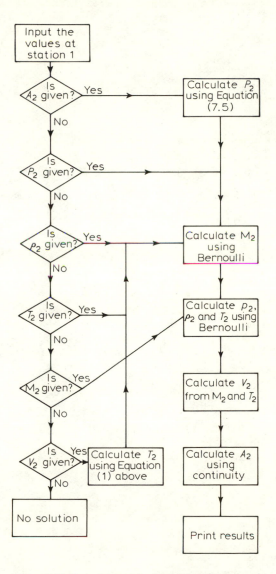

Figure 7.11 Flow diagram for FLOWDUCT Program

```
10      DIM Y(6)
20      PRINT "PLEASE INPUT VALUES OF GAS VELOCITY, PRESSURE, TEMPERATURE(DEG K)"
30      PRINT "  AND DUCT CROSS SECTIONAL AREA AT STATION 1 IN SI UNITS"
40      INPUT V1,P1,T1,A1
50      PRINT V1,P1,T1,A1
60      PRINT
70      D1=P1/(287*T1)
80      Ss1=20.04*SQR(T1)
90      M1=V1/Ss1
100     Ps=P1*(1+M1*M1/5)^3.5
110     Ts=T1*(1+M1*M1/5)
120     Ds=Ps/(287*Ts)
130     Md=D1*A1*V1
140     DATA "A2 (DUCT AREA)","P2 (PRESSURE)","D2 (DENSITY)","T2 (TEMPERATURE)","M
2 (MACH NUMBER)","V2 (VELOCITY)"
150     FOR N=1 TO 6
160       READ B$
170       GOSUB 700
180       IF N=1 THEN 280
190       IF N=2 THEN 380
200       IF N=3 THEN 410
210       IF N=4 THEN 440
220       IF N=5 THEN 470
230       IF N=6 THEN 490
240     NEXT N
250     PRINT
260     PRINT "NO INFORMATION AVAILABLE AT STATION 2. END OF PROGRAMME"
270     GOTO 780
280     A2=X
290     C=(Md/A2)^2/(7*Ps*Ds)
300     Pr=1
310     F=C-Pr^(10/7)+Pr^(12/7)
320     Df=-10/7*Pr^(3/7)+12/7*Pr^(5/7)
330     Pr=Pr-F/Df
340     IF ABS(F/Df)<.0001 THEN 360
350     GOTO 310
360     P2=Pr*Ps
370     GOTO 390
380     P2=X
390     M2=SQR(((Ps/P2)^(1/3.5)-1)*5)
400     GOTO 520
410     D2=X
420     M2=SQR(((Ds/D2)^(1/2.5)-1)*5)
430     GOTO 520
440     T2=X
450     M2=SQR(5*(Ts/T2-1))
460     GOTO 520
470     M2=X
480     GOTO 520
490     V2=X
500     T2=Ts-V2*V2/(7*287)
510     GOTO 450
520     Y(5)=M2
530     P2=Ps/(1+M2*M2/5)^3.5
540     Y(2)=P2
550     D2=Ds/(1+M2*M2/5)^2.5
560     Y(3)=D2
570     T2=Ts/(1+M2*M2/5)
580     Y(4)=T2
590     V2=M2*20.04*SQR(T2)
600     Y(6)=V2
610     A2=Md/(D2*V2)
620     Y(1)=A2
630     RESTORE
640     PRINT
650     FOR N=1 TO 6
660       READ B$
670       PRINT B$;" = ";Y(N)
680     NEXT N
690     GOTO 780
700       PRINT "IS ";B$;" GIVEN? Y OR N    ";
710       INPUT A$
720       PRINT A$
730       IF A$="N" THEN 240
740       PRINT "WHAT IS ITS VALUE?   ";
750       INPUT X
760       PRINT X
770       RETURN
780     END
```

```
RUN
PLEASE INPUT VALUES OF GAS VELOCITY, PRESSURE, TEMPERATURE(DEG K)
  AND DUCT CROSS SECTIONAL AREA AT STATION 1 IN SI UNITS
 204       100000     288        .5

IS A2 (DUCT AREA) GIVEN? Y OR N     N
IS P2 (PRESSURE) GIVEN? Y OR N     N
IS D2 (DENSITY) GIVEN? Y OR N     N
IS T2 (TEMPERATURE) GIVEN? Y OR N     N
IS M2 (MACH NUMBER) GIVEN? Y OR N     Y
WHAT IS ITS VALUE?    .8

A2 (DUCT AREA) = .436823019086
P2 (PRESSURE) = 83665.3872362
D2 (DENSITY) = 1.06512653731
T2 (TEMPERATURE) = 273.692390986
M2 (MACH NUMBER) = .8
V2 (VELOCITY) = 265.22781408


RUN
PLEASE INPUT VALUES OF GAS VELOCITY, PRESSURE, TEMPERATURE(DEG K)
  AND DUCT CROSS SECTIONAL AREA AT STATION 1 IN SI UNITS
 250       80000     400        1

IS A2 (DUCT AREA) GIVEN? Y OR N     N
IS P2 (PRESSURE) GIVEN? Y OR N     Y
WHAT IS ITS VALUE?    100000

A2 (DUCT AREA) = 2.17291847258
P2 (PRESSURE) = 100000
D2 (DENSITY) = .817277488752
T2 (TEMPERATURE) = 426.332623307
M2 (MACH NUMBER) = .237084487215
V2 (VELOCITY) = 98.1013850005
```

Program notes

(1) Line 10 declares dimensions of a six element array, Y; it will be used to store output data.

(2) Lines 20 to 50 input and print four independent flow parameters at station 1 (other sets of four could, of course, have been used) and lines 70 to 130 calculate density, D1, speed of sound, Ss1, Mach number, M1, stagnation pressure, density and temperature, Ps, Ds and Ts, and mass flow rate, Md; these latter values are not printed but could easily be, if required.

(3) Line 140 contains six string variable data items; these will be READ and used twice in the subsequent program – first, at lines 160 and 700 (in the subroutine) when information on conditions at station 2 is being sought and, secondly, at lines 660 (after the RESTORE at 630) and 670 when output is being printed.

(4) The FOR loop from 150 to 240 requests information (using the SUBROUTINE at line 700) on the flow parameter specified at station 2. The value is input initially as X, and the program then jumps (depending on the current value of N) to the next appropriate statement at 280, 380, 410, 440, 470 or 490, where X is converted into a flow parameter. Note that, in some versions of

BASIC, the six conditional statements from 180 to 230 could be replaced by a single line, which will be similar to:

ON N GOTO 280, 380, 410, 440, 470, 490

This causes the program to jump to the Nth of the specified lines, e.g. if N is currently 4, the program goes to line 440.

(5) Lines 280 to 620 calculate flow parameters at station 2 according to the flow diagram in Figure 7.11. Lines 290 to 350 calculate Pr (Pressure ratio, P_2/p_s) from A2 using a Newton-Raphson iteration to solve Equation (7.5), the St Venant equation; line 360 converts pressure ratio into P2. Flow parameters, when finally calculated, are stored in array Y, e.g. line 580 stores T2 in Y(4).

(6) The RESTORE statement at line 630 causes the next subsequent READ statement (line 660) to return to the first item of the string variables stored in the DATA statement at line 140.

(7) Lines 650 to 680 print results using string variables from the READ/DATA statements, and numeric variables stored in array Y.

(8) The SUBROUTINE from 700 to 770 enquires which flow variable is specified at station 2, and inputs its value as X.

(9) The two RUNs are routine; students should experiment to investigate conditions at points of interest in duct flow, e.g. (1) conditions near a throat where M = 1, (2) limiting supersonic conditions as M tends to infinity and (3) stagnation conditions.

Example 7.2   MACHMETER: tabulation of corresponding values of Mach number and pressure ratio in the calibration equation of the Machmeter

The flight instrument for measuring aircraft Mach number uses pressures obtained from a pitot tube and from a static vent which senses atmospheric static pressure. At speeds below the speed of sound, the ratio of these two pressures is related to Mach number by Equation (2.18):

$$\frac{P_{ST}}{P} = \left(1 + \frac{M^2}{5} \right)^{3.5} \qquad \text{for air}$$

This is the subsonic calibration equation.

At supersonic speeds, the pitot pressure recorded, P_{ST_2}, is the pressure downstream of a normal shock through which the air must pass before entering the pitot tube. This is related to the stagnation pressure, P_{ST}, entering the pitot tube. This is related to the stagnation pressure, P_{ST}, upstream of the shock and Mach number, M, by Equations (7.14) and (7.12) with $\theta = \pi/2$. The supersonic calibration Equation is therefore

$$\frac{P_{ST_2}}{P} = \frac{P_{ST_2}}{P_{ST_1}} \frac{P_{ST_1}}{P} = \frac{166.9 M^7}{(7M^2 - 1)^{2.5}} \qquad \text{for air}$$

This is Rayleigh's equation. The two calibration equations are continuous through the transonic speed range, both giving a pressure ratio of 1.893 at M = 1.

The following program tabulates the Mach number of pressure ratios ranging from 1 to 10.

```
10      PRINT
20      PRINT "PRESSURE RATIO          MACH NUMBER"
30      PRINT "--------------          -----------"
40      PRINT
50      IMAGE 4X,DD.D,19X,D.DD
60      FOR P=1 TO 10 STEP .5
70        IF P>2 THEN 170
80        FOR P0=P TO P+.41 STEP .1
90          Pr=P0
100         IF P0>1.893 THEN 130
110         GOSUB Sub
120         GOTO 140
130         GOSUB Super
140         PRINT USING 50;P0,M
150       NEXT P0
160       GOTO 200
170       Pr=P
180       GOSUB Super
190     PRINT USING 50;P,M
200     NEXT P
210     GOTO 310
220 Sub:    !
230       M=SQR(5*(Pr^(1/3.5)-1))
240     RETURN
250 Super:  !
260       F=166.9*M^7-Pr*(7*M*M-1)^2.5
270       F1=1168.3*M^6-Pr*35*M*(7*M*M-1)^1.5
280       M=M-F/F1
290       IF ABS(F/F1)>.002 THEN 260
300     RETURN
310     END


RUN

PRESSURE RATIO          MACH NUMBER
--------------          -----------
       1.0                  0.00
       1.1                   .37
       1.2                   .52
       1.3                   .62
       1.4                   .71
       1.5                   .78
       1.6                   .85
       1.7                   .90
       1.8                   .96
       1.9                  1.00
```

2.0	1.05
2.1	1.09
2.2	1.13
2.3	1.16
2.4	1.20
2.5	1.23
3.0	1.39
3.5	1.52
4.0	1.65
4.5	1.76
5.0	1.87
5.5	1.97
6.0	2.07
6.5	2.16
7.0	2.25
7.5	2.33
8.0	2.42
8.5	2.50
9.0	2.57
9.5	2.65
10.0	2.72

Program notes

(1) The program is required to tabulate values of M at pressure ratios ranging from 1 to 2.5 at intervals of 0.1, and from 2.5 to 10 at intervals of 0.5. Two FOR loops are used to achieve this. The outer loop from line 60 to line 200 starts at pressure ratio P = 1 and increments P in steps of 0.5; the inner loop from 80 to 150 starts at pressure ratio P0 = P and increments P0 in steps of 0.1, but this loop is bypassed by line 70 if P is greater than 2.

(2) In line 80, the final value of P0 is given as (P0 + 0.41), and not (P0 + 0.4), to ensure that rounding errors do not exclude the final desired value of (P0 + 0.4).

(3) Line 100 sends the program to one of two subroutines, labelled Sub and Super, depending on whether the pressure ratio is less than, or greater than, the sonic value of 1.893. It is often convenient to label subroutines with an appropriate name and to call them, by name, as shown in lines 110, 130 and also 180. The program would work equally well however if the subroutines were called by line number, i.e. GOSUB 230 and GOSUB 260, in which case lines 220 and 250 are not required. Before branching to either subroutine, Pr is set to the current value of the pressure ratio at lines 90 or 170.

(4) Lines 140 and 190 print results using the IMAGE statement at line 50 to control spacing and decimal places.

(5) The subroutine 'Super' uses the Newton–Raphson method to solve Rayleigh's equation; the starting value of M is the value at the end of the previous calculation.

Example 7.3   DOUBLEWED: a comparison of supersonic aerofoil theories

In Section 7.5, three methods of calculating surface pressure and force coefficients in supersonic flow were outlined: Ackeret, Busemann and shock expansion. This program compares the results of these three theories when applied to a symmetrical double wedge aerofoil over a range of incidences from 1 to 8°. surfaces are labelled as shown in Figure 7.12.

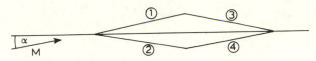

Figure 7.12 Double wedge aerofoil

```
10      DIM D(4),Cp(4),Pr(4),M1(4)
20      DATA "ACKERET","BUSEMANN","SHOCK-EXP"
30      PRINT "PLEASE INPUT THE FREE STREAM MACH NUMBER    ";
40      INPUT M
50      PRINT M
60      B=SQR(M*M-1)
70      C1=2/B
80      C2=(2.4*M^4-4*M^2+4)/(2*B^4)
90      PRINT "PLEASE INPUT THE DOUBLE WEDGE THICKNESS/CHORD RATIO    ";
100     INPUT T
110     PRINT T
120     PRINT USING "26A,DD.DD,8A";"DOUBLE WEDGE SEMI ANGLE = ";T*180/PI;" DEGREES
        "
130     PRINT
140     T1=ATN(T)
150     A1=PI/180
160     PRINT "INCIDENCE(DEG) = ";A1*180/PI;
170      D(1)=T1-A1
180      D(2)=T1+A1
190      D(3)=-T1-A1
200      D(4)=-T1+A1
210     PRINT ".   INCLINATIONS OF SURFACES TO FREESTREAM ARE (DEG):-"
220     PRINT USING "10X,#"
230     FOR N=1 TO 4
240       PRINT USING "DDD.DD,X,#";D(N)*180/PI  ;
250     NEXT N
260     PRINT
270     PRINT
280     PRINT "              CP(1)   CP(2)   CP(3)  CP(4)     CZ     CX     CL
CD     XCP"
290     FOR K=1 TO 3
300       FOR N=1 TO 4
310         IF K=1 THEN GOSUB Ackeret
320         IF K=2 THEN GOSUB Busemann
330         IF K=3 THEN GOSUB Sh_exp
340       NEXT N
350       GOSUB Coeff
360       READ Method$
370       GOSUB Print
380     NEXT K
390     RESTORE
400     PRINT
410     PRINT
420     A1=2*A1
430     IF A1<PI/18 THEN 160
440     GOTO 980
450 Ackeret:    !
460         Cp(N)=2*D(N)/B
470     RETURN
480 Busemann:   !
490         Cp(N)=C1*D(N)+C2*D(N)*D(N)
500     RETURN
```

```
510 Sh_exp:      !
520          IF N=1 AND D(1)>0 THEN GOSUB Shock
530          IF N=1 AND D(1)<=0 THEN GOSUB Exp
540          IF N=2 THEN GOSUB Shock
550          IF N=3 OR N=4 THEN GOSUB Exp
560          GOTO 870
570 Shock:      !
580          Th=.1
590          F=TAN(D(N))*(M*M*(1.4+COS(2*Th))+2)-M*M*SIN(2*Th)+2/TAN(Th)
600          F1=-TAN(D(N))*2*M*M*SIN(2*Th)-2*M*M*COS(2*Th)-2/(SIN(Th)*SIN(Th))
610          Th=Th-F/F1
620          IF ABS(F/F1)>.00001 THEN 590
630          Pr(N)=(2.8*M*M*SIN(Th)*SIN(Th)-.4)/2.4
640          Cp(N)=(Pr(N)-1)/(.7*M*M)
650          M1(N)=SQR((.4*M*M*SIN(Th)*SIN(Th)+2)/((2.8*M*M*SIN(Th)*SIN(Th)-.4
)*SIN(Th-D(N))*SIN(Th-D(N))))
660          RETURN
670 Exp:        !
680          IF N=1 THEN 730
690          De=-2*T1
700          Mu=M1(N-2)
710          Pru=Pr(N-2)
720          GOTO 760
730           De=D(1)
740           Mu=M
750           Pru=1
760          Nuu=2.449*ATN(SQR((Mu*Mu-1)/6))-ATN(SQR(Mu*Mu-1))
770          Nud=Nuu-De
780          Md=Mu
790          F=Nud-2.449*ATN(SQR((Md*Md-1)/6))+ATN(SQR(Md*Md-1))
800          F1=-6*Md/(SQR(Md*Md-1)*(Md*Md+5))+1/(Md*SQR(Md*Md-1))
810          Md=Md-F/F1
820          IF ABS(F/F1)>.00001 THEN 790
830          M1(N)=Md
840          Pr(N)=Pru*((1+Mu*Mu/5)/(1+Md*Md/5))^3.5
850          Cp(N)=(Pr(N)-1)/(.7*M*M)
860          RETURN
870    RETURN
880 Coeff:      !
890          Cz=(-Cp(1)+Cp(2)-Cp(3)+Cp(4))*COS(T1)/2
900          Cx=(Cp(1)+Cp(2)-Cp(3)-Cp(4))*SIN(T1)/2
910          Cl=Cz*COS(Al)-Cx*SIN(Al)
920          Cd=Cz*SIN(Al)+Cx*COS(Al)
930          Xcp=(-Cp(1)+Cp(2)+3*(-Cp(3)+Cp(4)))*COS(T1)/(8*Cz)
940    RETURN
950 Print:      !
960          PRINT USING "10A,4(D.DDDD,X),X,5(2X,D.DDDD)";Method$,Cp(1),Cp(2),Cp(3
),Cp(4),Cz,Cx,Cl,Cd,Xcp
970    RETURN
980    END
RUN
PLEASE INPUT THE FREE STREAM MACH NUMBER    2.2
PLEASE INPUT THE DOUBLE WEDGE THICKNESS/CHORD RATIO    .04
DOUBLE WEDGE SEMI ANGLE =  2.29 DEGREES

INCIDENCE(DEG) =   1 .  INCLINATIONS OF SURFACES TO FREESTREAM ARE (DEG):-
            1.29   3.29  -3.29  -1.29

            CP(1)  CP(2)  CP(3)  CP(4)       CZ      CX      CL      CD      XCP
ACKERET     .0230  .0586 -.0586 -.0230     .0356   .0033   .0355   .0039   .5000
BUSEMANN    .0237  .0632 -.0540 -.0223     .0356   .0033   .0355   .0039   .4729
SHOCK-EXP   .0237  .0634 -.0542 -.0223     .0358   .0033   .0357   .0039   .4730

INCIDENCE(DEG) =   2 .  INCLINATIONS OF SURFACES TO FREESTREAM ARE (DEG):-
             .29   4.29  -4.29   -.29

            CP(1)  CP(2)  CP(3)  CP(4)       CZ      CX      CL      CD      XCP
ACKERET     .0052  .0764 -.0764 -.0052     .0712   .0033   .0710   .0057   .5000
BUSEMANN    .0052  .0842 -.0687 -.0051     .0712   .0033   .0710   .0057   .4729
SHOCK-EXP   .0052  .0846 -.0690 -.0051     .0716   .0033   .0714   .0058   .4730

INCIDENCE(DEG) =   4 .  INCLINATIONS OF SURFACES TO FREESTREAM ARE (DEG):-
           -1.71   6.29  -6.29   1.71

            CP(1)  CP(2)  CP(3)  CP(4)       CZ      CX      CL      CD      XCP
ACKERET    -.0304  .1121 -.1121  .0304     .1424   .0033   .1418   .0132   .5000
BUSEMANN   -.0292  .1288 -.0954  .0317     .1424   .0033   .1418   .0132   .4729
SHOCK-EXP  -.0292  .1300 -.0965  .0318     .1437   .0033   .1431   .0133   .4731
```

```
INCIDENCE(DEG) =   8 .  INCLINATIONS OF SURFACES TO FREESTREAM ARE (DEG):-
               -5.71  10.29 -10.29   5.71

             CP(1)  CP(2)  CP(3)  CP(4)    CZ     CX     CL     CD     XCP
ACKERET    -.1017  .1833 -.1833  .1017   .2848  .0033  .2816  .0429  .5000
BUSEMANN   -.0879  .2280 -.1386  .1155   .2848  .0033  .2816  .0429  .4729
SHOCK-EXP  -.0888  .2337 -.1435  .1169   .2912  .0034  .2879  .0439  .4734
```

Program notes

(1) Lines 30 to 140 input freestream Mach number, M, and wedge thickness chord ratio, T, and calculate Ackeret and Busemann coefficients C1 and C2, and wedge nose semi-angle, T1. Line 150 sets incidence at 1° and lines 170 to 250 calculate and print the inclinations D(N) of the four surfaces to the freestream direction. The # symbol in the PRINT USING statements suppresses the normal carriage return/line feed.

(2) Lines 290 to 380 contain a FOR loop which successively calculates the four Ackeret, Busemann and shock expansion surface pressure coefficients using subroutines in the loop from 300 to 340. From these values, line 350 finds the force coefficients and centre of pressure position using the subroutine coefficient, and line 370 prints the results – again by subroutine. The subroutines are labelled and called by label for convenience; they could have been called by line number, e.g. GOSUB 460 instead of GOSUB Ackeret. Line 420 doubles the incidence and, provided it is less than 10, the program is returned to line 160.

(3) The Ackeret and Busemann subroutines apply the previously calculated coefficients and surface flow deflection angles to Equations (7.21) and (7.25). The shock expansion subroutine first decides (lines 520 to 550) whether there is a shock or expansion at the leading edge of each surface and the appropriate subroutine Shock or Expansion is then entered.

(4) The Shock subroutine solves Equation (7.9) for shock angle, Th, at given deflection angle and Mach number, using a Newton-Raphson iteration from 580 to 620. Once Th is found, the surface pressure ratio (relative to freestream pressure) is calculated at 630 using Equation (7.10) and pressure coefficient follows. Local Mach number, M1(N), is found at 650 because it will be needed in subsequent calculations on the expansions at the 1/3 and 2/4 corners.

(5) The Expansion subroutine first determines the flow deflection angle, De, upstream Mach number, Mu and upstream pressure ratio, Pru. Then, 760 calculates upstream Nu (Nuu) from Equation (7.18), 770 calculates downstream Nu (Nud) from Equation (7.17) and 780 to 820 contain a Newton-Raphson solution to Equation (7.18) for downstream Mach number, Md. Then downstream pressure ratio is calculated using Equation (7.18) and Cp follows.

(6) The coefficient subroutine uses surface pressure coefficients, resolved in appropriate directions, to calculate normal force, axial force, lift and drag coefficients. Xcp is the distance of the centre of pressure from the leading edge as a fraction of chord.

(7) A RUN at M = 2.2 and t/c = 0.04 is shown. Note the exact agreement of Ackeret and Busemann force coefficient values although the individual surface pressures are different. At the low incidences considered, the axial force is the same at all incidences, being a function of thickness distribution only. The drag coefficient, however, is dependent both on the axial force and on a lift induced component. Centre of pressure position is at mid-chord according to Ackeret but the other two more accurate theories place it slightly ahead of this point.

Example 7.4   TIPEFFECT: calculations on the pressure distribution within the tip Mach triangle of a rectangular wing at supersonic speeds

On a supersonic rectangular wing, flow is conical within the triangular areas bounded by the Mach lines through the tip leading edges. In particular, the pressure difference (Δp) across upper and lower surfaces is constant along lines through the tip leading edge at angle θ to the wing edge and is expressed by Equation (7.46):

$$C_\theta = \frac{\Delta p}{\tfrac{1}{2}\gamma p M^2} = C \frac{2}{\pi} \sin^{-1} \left(\frac{\tan \theta}{\tan \mu}\right)^{1/2}$$

where C is the two-dimensional loading coefficient $= 4\alpha/(M^2 - 1)^{1/2}$.

This program inputs freestream Mach number and tabulates values of C_θ (as fractions of the two-dimensional value) over a range of values of θ. The program then finds the average loading over the tip triangle as a fraction of the two-dimensional value by numerical integration.

```
10      PRINT "PLEASE ENTER THE FREESTREAM MACH NUMBER   ";
20      INPUT M
30      PRINT M
40      Mu=ASN(1/M)
50      PRINT "MACH ANGLE = ";Mu*180/PI;
60      A=4/SQR(M*M-1)
70      PRINT ".    2 DIM LIFT CURVE SLOPE = ";A
80      PRINT "PLEASE ENTER THE NUMBER OF TRIANGULAR STRIPS INTO WHICH"
90      PRINT "   THE TIP MACH TRIANGLE IS TO BE DIVIDED   ";
100     INPUT NO
110     PRINT NO
120     PRINT
130     S=0
140     PRINT "ANGLE FROM TIP EDGE(DEG)      CP AS FRACTION OF 2-D VALUE"
150     IMAGE 5X,DD.DDD,25X,D.DDDD
160     PRINT USING 150;0,0
170     FOR N=1 TO NO
180        Cpf=2/PI*ASN(SQR(TAN(N*Mu/NO)/TAN(Mu)))
190        S=S+Cpf*Mu/(NO*COS(N*Mu/NO)*COS(N*Mu/NO))
200        IF N/10=INT(N/10) THEN PRINT USING 150;N*Mu*180/(PI*NO),Cpf
210     NEXT N
220     Cp=S/TAN(Mu)
230     PRINT "AVERAGE LOADING OVER TIP MACH CONE IS ";Cp;" OF 2-D VALUE"
240     END
```

```
RUN
PLEASE ENTER THE FREESTREAM MACH NUMBER    2
MACH ANGLE =  30  .   2 DIM LIFT CURVE SLOPE =   2.30940107676
PLEASE ENTER THE NUMBER OF TRIANGULAR STRIPS INTO WHICH
    THE TIP MACH TRIANGLE IS TO BE DIVIDED    100

ANGLE FROM TIP EDGE(DEG)      CP AS FRACTION OF 2-D VALUE
        0.000                       0.0000
        3.000                        .1948
        6.000                        .2806
        9.000                        .3509
       12.000                        .4151
       15.000                        .4771
       18.000                        .5401
       21.000                        .6070
       24.000                        .6825
       27.000                        .7773
       30.000                       1.0000
AVERAGE LOADING OVER TIP MACH CONE IS  .506113625336   OF 2-D VALUE
```

Program notes

(1) Freestream Mach number, M, is input at line 20, and μ Mach angle, Mu, and two-dimensional wing lift curve slope, A, are calculated.

(2) Lines 80 to 110 input the number, NO, of intervals into which the Mach angle is to be divided, and line 180 calculates fractional pressure loadings along rays at angles θ ranging from 0 to μ at intervals of μ/NO. The tip Mach triangle is subdivided into NO triangular strips, each subtending angle μ/NO at the tip leading edge, and the loading on each strip is calculated (pressure $\times$ area) and added to an accumulated loading, S, at line 190. The average pressure loading, Cp, is then found at line 220 by dividing S by the tip triangular area which is proportional to tan μ.

(3) Line 200 permits only one in every ten calculated loading values to be printed. The PRINT USING output statements at lines 160 and 200 are controlled by the IMAGE statement at line

150. Line 230 outputs the average tip loading as a fraction of the two-dimensional value.

(4) One RUN is shown at M = 2, giving a Mach angle of 30°; this angle is divided into 100 intervals for calculation of conical loadings and for integration of the surface forces. As a result of numerical errors, the average tip triangle loading is found to be about 1% different from the theoretical value of 0.5 as quoted in the notes following Equation (7.46).

PROBLEMS

(7.1) Write a program which will input the stagnation temperature T_{st} (<1000 K) in a supersonic wind tunnel and tabulate the static temperature in the working section for an appropriate range of working section Mach numbers; print a cautionary message if this temperature goes below 100 K. Then, extend the program to input the stagnation pressure and thence calculate the working section Reynolds number per metre; Equations (2.4) and (2.5) may be used for speed of sound and viscosity of air.

(7.2) Write a program which will input stagnation pressure and temperature, and the Mach number of a supersonic flow in a duct where cross section is given, and which will then output the duct area where conditions would be sonic, followed by the pressure, temperature, density, speed of sound and mass flow rate at this point.

(7.3) Write a program which compares the pressure coefficients predicted by Ackeret, Busemann and shock-expansion theories at a specified point on the surface of a biconvex aerofoil of given thickness/chord ratio at zero incidence.

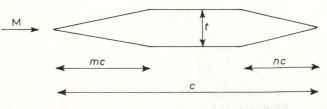

Figure 7.13 Modified double wedge aerofoil

(7.4) The modified double wedge aerofoil shown in Figure 7.13 is frequently used in missile wings. Write a program which, for a given Mach number and thickness/chord ratio, will calculate the Ackeret pressure coefficients on the four sloping faces at zero incidence, for a range of values of the fractions m and n between 0.2 and 0.8 ($m + n \leqslant 1$). Then evaluate the drag coefficient and finally tabulate these values so as to show that the minimum drag occurs when $m = n = 0.5$.

(7.5) At a fixed upstream Mach number M_1, Equation (7.9) has two solutions for shock angle θ at a given deflection angle δ, provided δ does not exceed the maximum value appropriate to M_1. Write a program which will input M_1 and calculate and tabulate these two shock angles for a range of deflection angles from 0 to δ_{max}. Then extend the program to find some of the other parameters downstream of the shock using Equations (7.10) to (7.14).

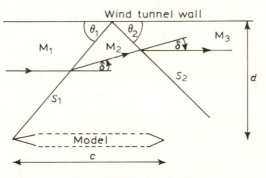

Figure 7.14 Shock reflection

(7.6) Simple shock reflection. If a flow parallel to plane solid surfaces (as in the working section of a supersonic wind tunnel) meets an oblique shock S_1 at angle θ_1, a flow deflection δ will occur. A reflected shock S_2 is generated from the point where S_1 meets the wall which must re-deflect the flow through the same deflection angle δ in order to restore a flow parallel to the surfaces. Write a program which will input M_1 and θ_1 and which will calculate and print Mach numbers M_2 and M_3, deflection angle δ and the second shock angle θ_2, assuming no further interactions with other model induced shocks or expansions. An appropriate message is to be printed if the flow deflection angle at S_2 is greater than the maximum associated with M_2. Then extend the program to input the model length, c and the tunnel dimension, d and to print a warning message if the reflected shock interferes with the model.

(**7.7**) Write a program which will input freestream Mach number and the aspect ratio of a rectangular wing and then calculate the loading coefficient at a specified point on the wing surface, using Equations (7.22) or (7.46). The program should be capable of dealing with any wing aspect ratio greater than $2 \tan \mu$ where μ is Mach angle.

(**7.8**) Equations (7.47) and (7.49) give expressions for the lift and drag coefficients of a supersonic rectangular wing. Write a program which will input Mach number and wing parameters, and then tabulate these coefficients and the lift/drag ratio over a range of incidences. Then extend the program to find the maximum lift/drag ratio and the incidence at which it occurs.

Bibliography

In addition to the books on BASIC listed in Section 1.5, the following are suggested further reading.

Allen, J. E., *Aerodynamics. The Science of Air in Motion*, 2nd ed., Granada, (1982).

Bertin, J. J. and Smith, M. L., *Aerodynamics for Engineers*, Prentice Hall, (1979).

Clancy, L. J., *Aerodynamics*, Pitman Books Ltd, (1975).

Curle, S. N. and Davies, H. J., *Modern Fluid Dynamics*, Van Nostrand Reinhold, (1971).

Duncan, W. J., Thom, A. S. and Young, A. D., *Mechanics of Fluids*, Edward Arnold, (1960).

Houghton, E. L. and Carruthers, N. B., *Aerodynamics for Engineering Students*, 3rd ed., Edward Arnold, (1982).

Krasnov, N. F., *Aerodynamics*, translated & published by NASA, (1978).

Kuethe, A. M. and Chow, C., *Foundations of Aerodynamics*, 3rd ed., John Wiley, (1976).

Massey, B. S., *Mechanics of Fluids*, 4th ed., Van Nostrand Reinhold, (1979).

Nielsen, J. N., *Missile Aerodynamics*, McGraw Hill, (1960).

Pankhurst, R. C. and Holder, D. W., *Wind Tunnel Technique*, Pitman Books Ltd, (1952).

Pope, A. and Harper, J. J., *Low-Speed Wind Tunnel Testing*, John Wiley, (1966).

Schlichting, H. S., *Boundary Layer Theory*, 6th ed., McGraw Hill, (1968).

Schreier, S., *Compressible Flow*, John Wiley, (1982).

Ward, G. N., *Linearised Theory of Steady High Speed Flow*, CUP, (1955).

Index

Butterworths BASIC Books

The Butterworths BASIC Books series is the first coherent series to link undergraduate studies with computer programming using the language BASIC – the simplest of all computer languages and the one which is spoken by virtually all micros. Each book demonstrates how computing methods can be used to solve real problems in its subject area, and the series as a whole is the first to promote the computer as a learning tool. Each book contains tested and practical computer programs but also encourages readers to develop their own programming. The books are suitable for undergraduates and practising engineers.

The series covers topics in:

Civil Engineering

Mechanical and Aeronautical Engineering

Mathematics and Statistics

Materials and Metallurgy

Full details of all titles in the series are available from

 Butterworths
Borough Green, Sevenoaks, Kent TN15 8PH